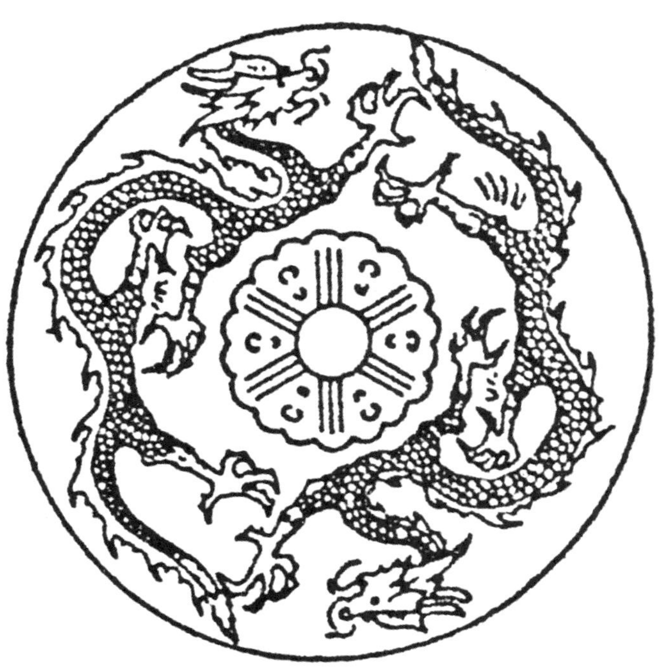

Yuan-dynasty four-clawed double dragon roundel

IMAGES OF ASIA

Chinese Dragons

TITLES IN THE SERIES

Arts of the Tang Court
PATRICA EICHENBAUM KARETZKY

At the Chinese Table
T.C. LAI

At the Japanese Table
RICHARD HOSKING

The Cheongsam
HAZEL CLARK

China's Muslims
MICHAEL DILLON

China's Walled Cities
RONALD G. KNAPP

Chinese Almanacs
RICHARD J. SMITH

Chinese Bridges
RONALD G. KNAPP

Chinese Classical Furniture
GRACE WU BRUCE

The Chinese Garden
JOSEPH CHO WANG

The Chinese House
RONALD G. KNAPP

Chinese Dragons
ROY BATES

Chinese Jade
JOAN HARTMAN-GOLDSMITH

Chinese Maps
RICHARD J. SMITH

Chinese Musical Instruments
ALAN R. THRASHER

Chinese Mythological Gods
KEITH G. STEVENS

Chinese New Year
PATRICIA BJAALAND WELCH

Chinese Painting
T.C. LAI

Chinese Paper Offerings
RODERICK CAVE

Chinese Snuff Bottles
ROBERT KLEINER

Chinese Tomb Figurines
ANN PALUDAN

The Forbidden City
MAY HOLDSWORTH

Japanese Cinema: An Introduction
DONALD RICHIE

The Japanese Kimono
HUGO MUNSTERBERG

Japanese Musical Instruments
HUGH DE FERRANTI

Korean Musical Instruments
KEITH HOWARD

Korean Painting
KEITH PRATT

Macau
CÉSAR GUILLÉN-NUÑEZ

Mandarin Squares: Mandarins and their Insignia
VALERY M. GARRETT

The Ming Tombs
ANN PALUDAN

Modern Chinese Art
DAVID CLARKE

New Chinese Cinema
KWOK-KAN TAM &
WIMAL DISSANAYAKE

Old Kyoto
JOHN LOWE

Old Seoul
KEITH PRATT

Old Shanghai
BETTY PEH-T'I WEI

Old Tokyo
KEIKO IMAI PACKARD

Peking Opera
COLIN MACKERRAS

South China Village Culture
JAMES HAYES

Temples of the Empress of Heaven
JOSEPH BOSCO & PUAY-PENG HO

Traditional Chinese Clothing
VALERY M. GARRETT

Series Editors, China Titles:
NIGEL CAMERON, SYLVIA FRASER-LU

Chinese Dragons

ROY BATES

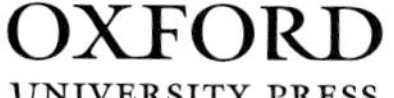
UNIVERSITY PRESS

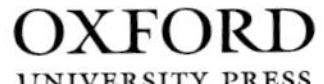

Oxford University Press is a department of the University of Oxford.
It furthers the University's objective of excellence in research, scholarship,
and education by publishing worldwide in

Oxford New York

Auckland Bangkok Buenos Aires Cape Town Chennai
Dar es Salaam Delhi Hong Kong Istanbul Karachi Kolkata
Kuala Lumpur Madrid Melbourne Mexico City Mumbai Nairobi
São Paulo Shanghai Singapore Taipei Tokyo Toronto

and an associated company in Berlin

Oxford is a registered trade mark of Oxford University Press

Published in the United States
by Oxford University Press Inc., New York

First published 2002
This impression (lowest digit)
1 3 5 7 9 10 8 6 4 2

British Library Cataloguing in Publication Data
available

Library of Congress Cataloging-in-Publication Data
available

ISBN 0-19-592856-3

Printed in Hong Kong
Published by Oxford University Press (China) Ltd
18th Floor, Warwick House East, Taikoo Place, 979 King's Road, Quarry Bay
Hong Kong

Contents

The dragon is the spirit of change, therefore of life itself, taking new forms according to its surroundings, yet never seen in its final shape. It is the great mystery itself. Hidden in the caverns of inaccessible mountains, or coiled in the unfathomed depth of the sea, he awaits the time when he slowly arouses himself into activity. He unfolds himself in the storm cloud. He washes his mane in the darkness of the seething whirlpools. His claws are the fork of lightning... His voice is heard in the hurricane... The dragon reveals himself only to vanish.

Okakura Kakuso, *Book of Tea*, 1906

Preface

THE DRAGON HAS been the symbol of China since ancient times and for many centuries has been considered immortal and omnipresent. It served as the emblem of monarchy and supreme power, yet the dragon has always belonged to the people. The Chinese dragon was considered to be exclusively a beneficent beast until the Buddhists introduced the view that there were also evil dragons—but the basic concept of a dragon in the mind of the populace was one of noble spiritual qualities that were unconquerable. Although it is a mythical creature, claims of dragon sightings have been made on many occasions, some as recently as 1920. No other creature in the world has had such a far-reaching influence on the minds of so many people.

This book attempts to foster a wider understanding of the Chinese dragon and the many forms it took. It is dedicated to the dragon and its many offshoots and variations, and gives details of what a dragon was, where it was used, and what it was called. It is hoped that the reader will become more acquainted with the dragon and gain a greater awareness of this magnificent beast. The treatise is intended to interest and please the serious student and the enthusiastic tourist alike.

All Chinese terms, including the names of people and places, have been rendered in the pinyin romanization. All photographs are my own, while I am indebted to three books in my collection from which I have taken the majority of line drawings and rubbings: *Dragon*, *Chinese Dragon Patterns*, and *Chinese Dragons: Graphics and Rubbings*. Two figures were taken from *Chinese Ornament* (Fig. 1.9) and *Dragon* (Fig. 2.3).

Several people have given me helpful advice and information, for which I am grateful. I would particularly like to thank Gabrielle Harris for her valuable comments and criticisms, and Mr Wang Chun Yao and Wendy Zhao who gave me much information about dragon folklore. Many thanks are also due to my courteous and considerate editor, Ms Carey Vail, with whom have I enjoyed working. Finally, I must thank my wife, who patiently put up with my long-term enthusiasm and dedication, and my non-stop discussion of the subject.

Any queries, comments, or suggestions would be gratefully received. Please email me at <royba@163.com>.

Roy Bates
Beijing, 2002

1
The Evolution of the Chinese Dragon

THERE HAS BEEN much speculation about the origin of the Chinese dragon. One suggestion is that the dragon derived from dinosaurs (Fig. 1.1). But dinosaurs vanished long before the concept of a dragon arose, and just because fossilized dinosaur bones were revered by the Chinese, and ground up for medicine, this has no relevance to the dragon's origin.

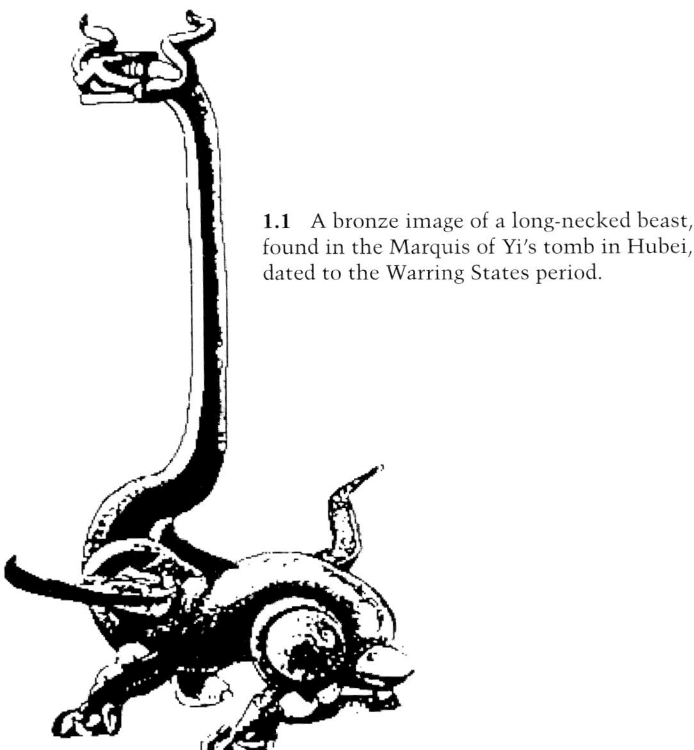

1.1 A bronze image of a long-necked beast, found in the Marquis of Yi's tomb in Hubei, dated to the Warring States period.

Snake-like figures have been found painted on pottery dated to the Shang dynasty (*c*.1700–1027 BC), which stimulated the theory that the dragon concept evolved from snakes (Fig. 1.2). However, the 'snakes' in the designs have little in common with dragons.

The proposition that dragons evolved from crocodiles is also popular (Fig. 1.3). Carved horizontal beasts found on walls of tombs also dated to the Shang dynasty, and a bronze vessel[1] unearthed at Taouhuazhuang, Shilou, Shanxi, roughly in the shape of a crocodile and also dated to the same period, tend to support the crocodile theory. While all have a long

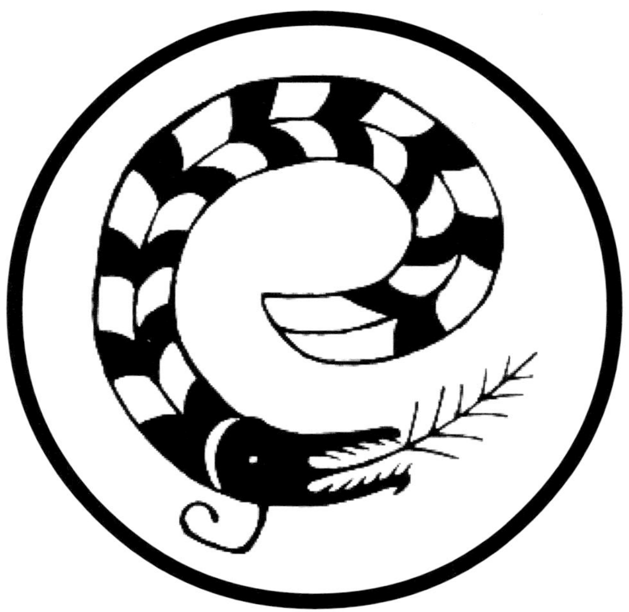

1.2 In early times a beast with the likeness of a water snake was revered, and appeared as jade talismans and as decoration on pottery.

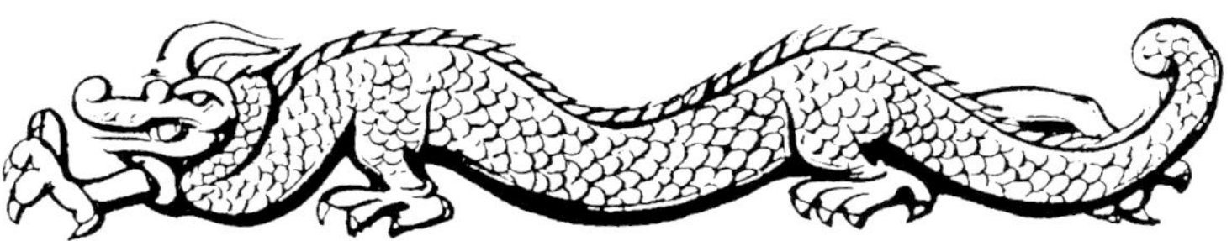

1.3 Examples of engravings of crocodile-shaped dragons are rare, but several examples have been found. This one is dated to the Song dynasty.

tapering body, the head has tufts of hair, and the protruding jaws are prominently curled at the ends. Some of the beasts on these carvings and bronzes have two feet and many authorities refer to them as *kui* dragons. More will be said about *kui* dragons later. Tombs dated to the Western Zhou period (*c.*1027–771 BC) also have carvings on stone walls that bear a superficial resemblance to *Crocodylidae*, but the beasts now have bottle-shaped horns and three claws on each foot. In some designs, the beast has protruding ridges along its back and on its belly. However, the crocodile has never been credited with magical powers and so this hypothesis does not hold water.

Interesting jade carvings in the shape of the letter C, with pig-like heads and smooth legless bodies, have been unearthed in tombs dated to the Hongshan culture (*c.*3500–2000 BC). It has been suggested that these are early dragons, but since most were found on the breasts of skeletons, they are probably talismans worn to protect from evil or to provide good fortune (Plate 1). Similar designs, in a simple inverted semicircular shape, have been discovered in Eastern Zhou dynasty tombs (770–221 BC) and are also probably talismans.

Carved jade artefacts found in tombs dated to the Warring States period (475–221 BC) bear a resemblance to a horse, but again these are probably talismans (Fig. 1.4). The scholar

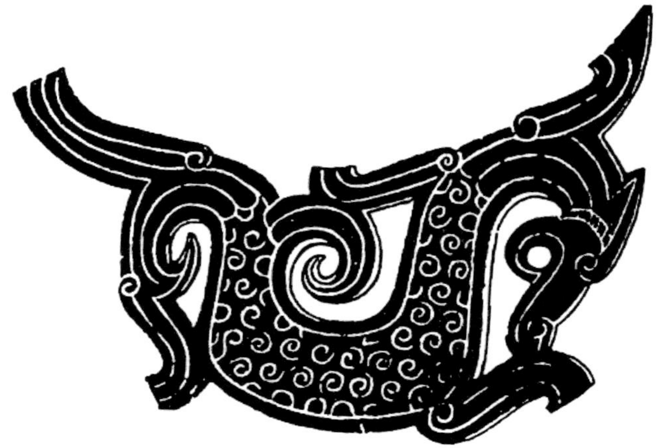

1.4 Many jades considered to be horse-headed dragons have been found in tombs dating to the Warring States period. They are usually pierced for wearing as talismans or decorative pendants.

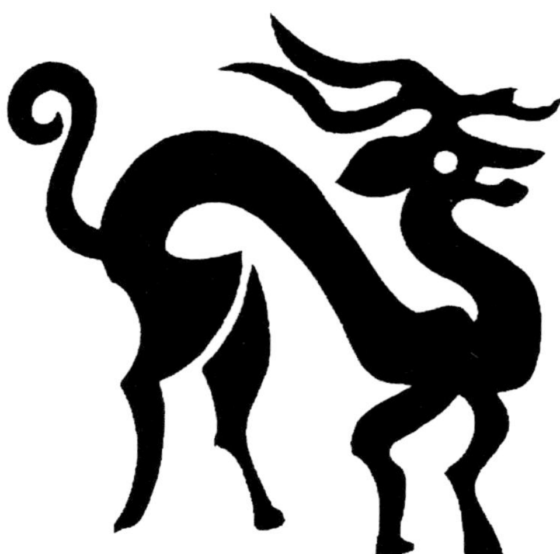

1.5 The dragon in very early times was often depicted with antlers like a stag.

Wang Fu (73–48 BC), a self-styled expert on dragons, wrote that, 'According to popular custom the dragon's shape was drawn with a horse's head and a snake's tail.' But he disagreed with this 'popular custom', and firmly stated that the head of a dragon was like that of a camel, with eyes like those of a devil, ears like those of an ox, and horns like those of a deer. He avowed that the neck was like that of a snake, the abdomen was like that of a large cockle, and the body had scales like those of a carp. The feet, he added, had claws like those of an eagle, though the soles were soft like those of a tiger. But where did he get his information? Possibly from the *Book of Plants and Animals* (*Er Ya Yi*), written around 1100 BC, which says that the dragon has a number of resemblances, namely horns that resemble the antlers of a stag (Fig. 1.5); a neck that resembles that of a snake; a belly, that of a cockle or a clam; scales like a carp's; talons like a hawk's; paws like a tiger's; and ears like those of an ox. It can be seen, therefore, that the dragon was made up of discrete parts of tangible animals. However, one can sympathize with a sculptor or an artist commissioned to depict a dragon with nothing to go by other than Wang Fu's delicious description. Historians have repeated these definitions many times as if they were gospel—however, it was not universally accepted at the time and several variations appeared over the years. Indeed, no examples of a dragon fitting this description have been unearthed that can be dated much before the birth of Christ. In fact, the scholar-writers, the painters, the sculptors, the designers of fabrics, and the embroiderers of robes each had their own view of what a dragon looked like, all generally similar to Wang Fu's version, but only superficially. Even so, it can be seen that by the last hundred years or so before the birth of Christ a general concept had emerged of what a dragon looked like.

In many respects the Chinese thought about dragons in the same way that children think about Father Christmas: to some he is Santa Claus; to others he is Saint Nicholas. In many places he comes on 24 December, but on a different day in others. In many places he mysteriously arrives down the chimney, but to those living without fireplaces he still manages to get in somehow. Every child who believes has some concept of him, but no one can be sure whether his beard is long and flowing or relatively short. He is a concept, a belief, a conviction, and he is not clear cut like Pooh Bear in *Winnie the Pooh*, who is the same in England as he is in America or anywhere else in the world. The Chinese looked upon dragons in the same way. They had palpable beasts like snakes, alligators, horses, and tigers that could be seen and studied, and their shape could be copied. Yet the dragon, like Father Christmas, was always intangible. Its shape, and its characteristics, varied from place to place. No one knew for certain what a dragon looked like, and it was not possible to go out into the wilds and see one.

Many dragon-like beasts emerged, some with two legs, others with four. Some dragons were depicted with a long tail that was bifurcated and flowing, as if it were some form of water plant, or perhaps elongated feathers. Sometimes this tail was bedecked with leaves (Fig. 1.6). This curious mixture of a faunistic and floral-tailed beast had a clear animal-like head and upper body, and many had only two legs. A beautiful scabbard slide in jade, dated to the Western Han dynasty (206 BC–AD 8), has been found where the beast has four sturdy legs on a sinuous body and a long, curling tail. There is a long and voluted plume flowing back from its head, sometimes assumed to be a horn. The face looks to the front, and could easily be taken for a cat or perhaps a tiger. Names were allocated to these curious beasts. In contrast to the *kui*

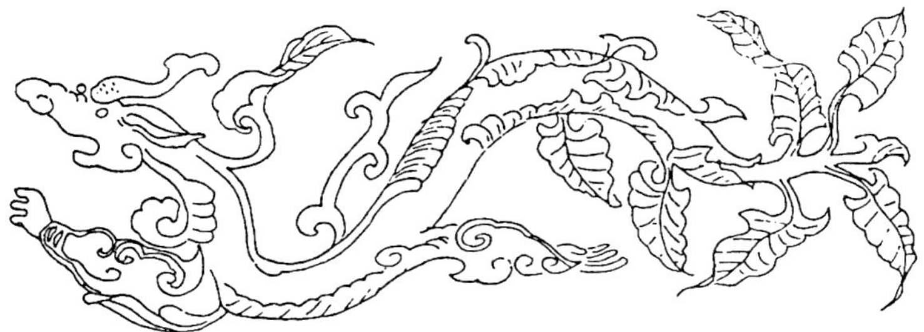

1.6 The dragon was depicted in many forms. Here in this Qing-dynasty image it is shown with a bifurcated tail and bedecked with leaves.

of the Shang period, which were almost exactly the same in shape but depicted with upturned noses, those with noses turned down were now called *kui* (Fig. 1.7), while those with noses curling upward were called *guaizi* (Fig. 1.8). The later Chinese historians insisted that these beasts were dragons, and largely because of a homophone of *guaizi* meaning 'noble sons' this dragon was often used to indicate a wish for such a blessing. *Kui* dragons carved in jade are usually shown in profile, and the Han-dynasty writer, Xu Shen (d.147), in his book, *Explanations of Principles for the Composition of Characters* (*Shuowen jiezi*), went so far as to state that the *kui* 'resembles a dragon with one leg'. Some have assumed that he was stating that the *kui* actually had one leg only. However, at the time these designs were carved, the understanding of perspective was limited and the probability is that the sculptor was not artistic enough to depict two legs. Even so, it is still widely stated that the *kui* had only one leg, even though examples of carvings of *kui* dragons with two legs have been found.

The opinion is sometimes voiced by Western historians that *kui* and *guaizi* are the Chinese version of the Hindu *makara*. But *makara* were water monsters that combined the

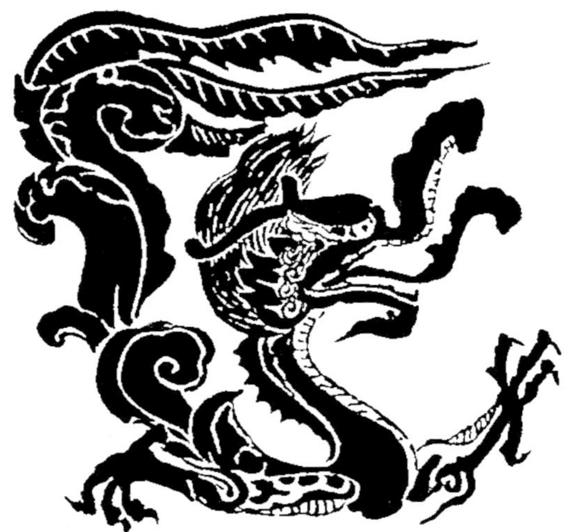

1.7 Qing-dynasty *kui* dragon design, a symbol of peace and good fortune, with downturned nose, two legs each with four claws, and a foliage tail.

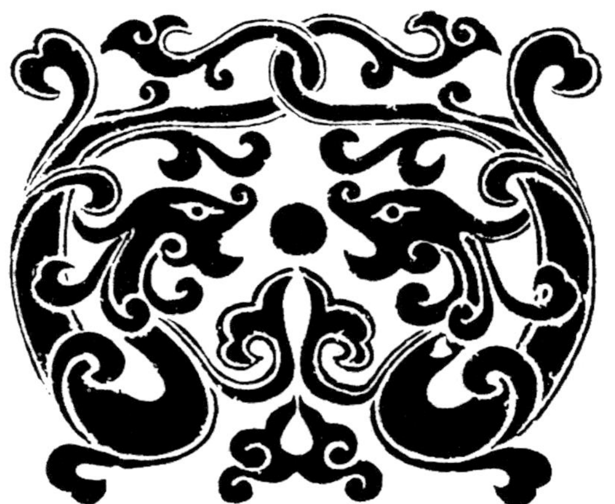

1.8 A pair of *guaizi* dragons with upturned noses, facing each other toward a central pearl. *Guaizi* are also often depicted facing a lotus or a lucky *shou* symbol of longevity.

head of an elephant with the body of a two-legged crocodile or serpent, or sometimes a fish. *Kui* certainly do not have elephantine heads—a trunk-like extension does protrude from beneath the nostrils, but it is more like an extended lip than a trunk. And unlike the elephant, *kui* have horns and are found where there is no logical connection with water, for example on the bases of steles erected to honour scholars who passed the official examinations with high honour, and on the bases of the decorative arch at the Ming Tombs near Beijing. Symbolically, *kui* dragons represented the source of life from which purity and perfection sprang, and denoted good fortune and peace. They never swam in dirty seas, and only drank the purest of water. They abhorred anything unclean and were fastidious in what they ate. I submit that their appearance on the base of steles to scholars passing high in the official examinations betokened purity, honesty, and lack of corruption, and that it was primarily to represent these noble characteristics that *kui* were also placed on the bases of the arch at the Ming Tombs, to honour the emperors and to wish them peace and good fortune.

Not all dragons had horns—hornless dragons were called *li*. By the Ming dynasty (1368–1644) there were hornless dragons called *chi*, considered to be immature, or young, dragons (Plate 2). The probability, however, is that *li* and *chi* were two names for the same dragon. They had long, flowery bifurcated tails, very much in the style of the *kui* and the *guaizi* dragons.

But there was little rein to the imagination of early writers. The Zhou-dynasty *Mountain and Water Classic* (*Shan Hai Jing*) solemnly pontificated about a special kind of dragon: 'Outside of the north sea, north of the red water, there is the Zhang Wei mountain, in which dwells a spirit with a human face and the body of a snake, and red staring eyes. When they close it is dark, when they are open it is light. This spirit does not eat or sleep. He does not breathe. Wind and rain obey his command. He lights up the deepest darkness. This spirit is called the candle dragon.' There are several others who referred to this candle dragon, notably Qu Yuan (*c.*340–278 BC), the unfortunate minister of King Zuo and one of the greatest poets of ancient China.[2] He wrote, 'When the sun has set and the traveller has not arrived at home, how can the candle dragon light his way?' Wang Yi, who lived around 130 AD, wrote, 'In the north-west there is a very dark country without a sun. A dragon holds a candle in its mouth and lights this country.' The official records of the Jin dynasty (265–420) stated, 'The Zhong He mountain, near the North Pole, is not illuminated by the sun and the moon. There is a green[3] dragon there, holding a lighted candle in its mouth to light up the four directions.' If you were a scholar in those days no one would dare to challenge such statements, nor question the source of your knowledge.

Many dragons could fly, and the *Book of Changes* (*Yi Jing*, often written as *I Ching*) refers to a flying dragon called 'nine-five', signifying its superiority as the expression 'the loftiness of nine and five' was synonymous with the imperial throne. Many examples of ceramics, tiles, and carved stone panels depicting dragons with bat-like wings have been found. In the early designs, the wings are more like three thin feathers, but by the fifteenth century the wings are more pronounced and bat-like in structure. The small but profusely illustrated Ming encyclopaedia, the *Collected Illustrations of the Three Realms* (*Sancai tuhui*), compiled by Wang Qi and his son Wang Siyi between 1607 and 1609, depicts a winged dragon and calls it a *ying long*. There was also a flying fish type of dragon called a *fei yü*, which was used on robes as a badge of honour (see Chapter 3). Many designs of winged beasts have been found so its concept was widespread. Several examples show winged beasts chasing fish, suggesting that they represent the dragon of the seas. Many sport primitive wing-like projections emerging from above the front haunches.

The *fei yü* is often confused with the fish-dragons found on the stone memorial arches known as *pai fang*. These creatures have an indisputable fish's body and they do have dragon-like heads, but they are *piao*, a name best translated as 'mark of distinction'.

Incidentally, there is also confusion between a *pai fang* and a *pai lou*. A *pai fang* is an honorary gate or archway erected for the purpose of indicating a specific mark of honour to an individual or a community, whereas a *pai lou* is a decorated monumental archway built to span a roadway used for imperial processions. The difference is easy to spot: *pai fang* have distinctive finials in the shape of a fish with a dragon's head mounted on them, *pai lou* do not.

The explanation for the presence of *piao* fish-dragons on honorary arches and gates is simple. A legend grew up that carp that leaped over the rapids of the Yellow River at the Dragon's Gate (Longmen) in the Hejing district, Shanxi, on the third moon of each year had their heads burned off by lightning and their faces were replaced by a dragon's face marked on their foreheads to distinguish them from the others. The long struggle of these fish against the rapids, and their eventual success in leaping over them, became synonymous with the long struggle of the literary scholar who eventually achieved success after much persistence and exertion. Thus, a fish-dragon in the shape of a carp with a dragon's face became the symbol of someone who had passed an examination for a degree with distinction. He was referred to as a 'carp that had leaped over the Dragon's Gate'.

The honour of erecting a *pai fang* gateway was granted to those worthy of special mention, a chaste widow, for example. It could also be granted to temples or even towns to signify honour to the citizens. Scholars who passed the official examinations with distinction were granted permission to put *piao* fish-dragons on the crosspieces that formed the lintels of arches. They might also be given a plate, or perhaps a vase, decorated with one or more *piao* fish-dragons—several exquisite silver plates decorated in gilt with this design have been found (Fig. 1.9).

In the first century BC another beast emerged. Brick tiles found in the Maolong tomb of the Emperor Wudi of the Western Han dynasty show a four-legged beast with long legs on a thin body, rather like a greyhound, and a long, thin tiger-like tail (Fig. 1.10). The head was elongated and had two horns. Similar designs have sometimes been found with markings on the beast's back, though they cannot be described as scales. Later, Chinese historians called this beast a *cang* dragon.

Yet another type of dragon has been found—a tile unearthed in what is believed to be a Han-dynasty tomb shows another style of dragon known as a *jiao*. This has four legs and its feet appear to have two claws. It has a long, beautiful curved body with curly tufts and an elongated, horned head with an extended snout curling upward, and was believed to live in the marshes (Fig. 1.11). One tile, now in the Nelson-Atkins Museum of Art in Kansas City, Missouri, in the United States, shows a human-shaped figure, probably an immortal, riding on the dragon's back. Several other *jiao* dragon designs have been found on tiles, but without a rider. The *jiao* was sometimes known as the flood dragon, for it was believed to cause flooding. However, it was considered to be a beneficent creature that exerted a

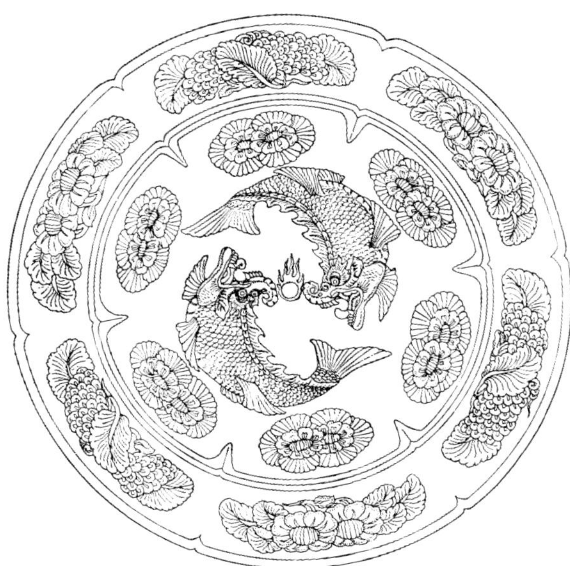

1.9 The fish-dragon, with the body of a carp and face of a dragon, was a symbol of literary eminence. Scholars who had passed examinations with distinction were often given gifts such as a plate decorated with one or more of these fish-dragons.

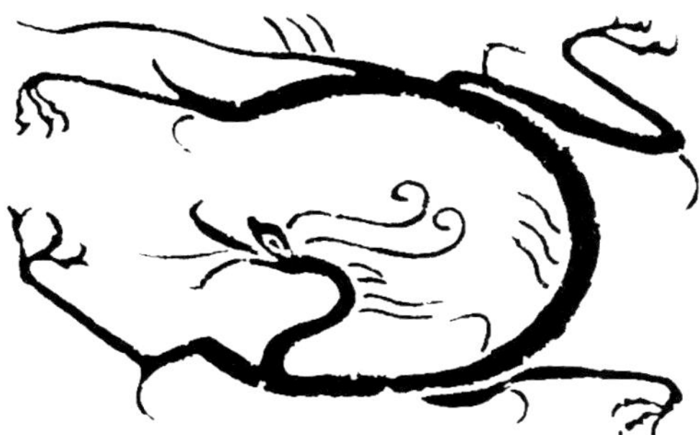

1.10 A rubbing of a four-legged dragon found in the tomb of the Emperor Wudi with a long thin tail, an elongated head, and two horns. This style of dragon was later referred to as a *cang* dragon.

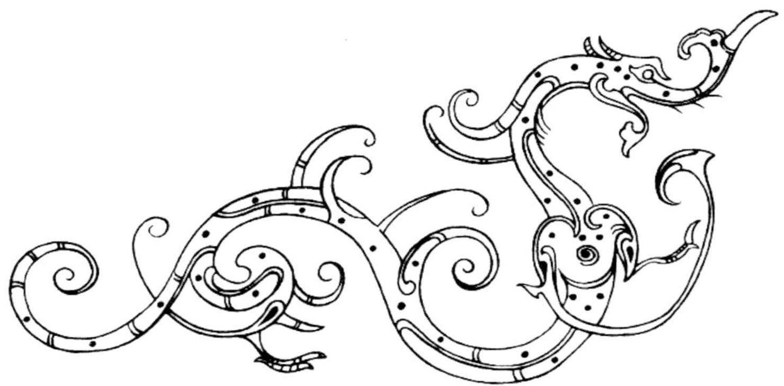

1.11 The *jiao* dragon, also known as the flood dragon, was believed to live in marshes. It had four legs, two claws on each foot, a long sinuous body, and an elongated head with upturned snout.

restraining influence against the sin of greed. Because of this, *jiao* often appeared in a highly conventional form on ancient Chinese bronzes associated with the preparation of food. In art and decoration, they were given a red breast and striped green and yellow sides.

Belief in four new kinds of powerful dragons, known as *long* dragons, now materialized. They all inhabited the sky but had differing duties. One of these, called *tian long* or heavenly dragons, acted as a kind of praetorian guard to protect the mansions of the gods. Another, known as *shen long* or spirit dragons, had the duty of producing rain for the benefit of mankind. The responsibility for marking out the courses of rivers and streams was allocated to the *di long*, the dragons of the earth. The fourth duty, namely to guard and watch over the heavenly wealth concealed from mortal eyes, was undertaken by the *cang long*, the dragons of hidden treasures (no connection with *cang* dragons). Several *cang long* designs have been found on tiles and on light relief stone panels with dragons being ridden by immortals.

By the time of the Song dynasty (960–1279) dragons were beginning to look more like we understand them today. There were further amendments during the Yuan dynasty (1279–1368), but it was the first Ming emperor, Hongwu, who demanded that the design be refined and standardized and it now matured to its full glory, splendid and imperialistic (Plate 3). Yet although it had its own characteristics and features, like Father Christmas it was still only a concept, a belief, a conviction, and was never a real beast.

Notes

1 This is a ritual vessel called a *dong,* probably used for holding a liquid such as oil for anointing. Vessels of this sort are shaped like a sauce boat, usually with a separate lid. Either the lid or the spout of the vessel is designed in the shape of an animal head.

2 After realizing that he could not influence his sovereign to desist from evil ways nor eliminate governmental corruption, Qu Yuan committed suicide on the fifth day of the fifth moon of the Chinese lunar calendar by jumping into the river holding a large stone. The people, who respected his fidelity and virtue, sent out boats in search of his body, but failed. Each year thereafter to honour Qu Yuan's soul, boats would be put out on the river and it is this practice that developed into the Dragon Boat Festival, though why the boats were considered 'dragon boats' is not known.

3 The word in Chinese for this colour can be variously translated as green, blue, or azure. While it is conventional to use the term azure, in this book the word 'green' is used to signify this colour.

2
The Dragon: Ours, His, or Theirs?

NOWADAYS MOST people consider the dragon to be an imperial emblem. But it was not always so. The dragon, as a concept of a powerful spirit, existed in the minds of the common people as far back as can be discovered, although this concept varied from time to time and from place to place. A description of the dragon given in the 1100 BC *Book of Plants and Animals*, later modified by Wang Fu, was extended by popular consent. By 100 BC the dragon was considered to have whiskers on each side of its mouth, a beard under its chin where a bright flaming pearl could be found, and scales—those on the throat were now said to lie towards the head. The scales on the head became disposed like the ridges in a chain of mountains and there were eighty-one ridge-like scales along its back. The tellers of tales added more details. Its breath, it was said, came out of its mouth like a cloud, which sometimes changed into water, but at other times it breathed fire. It ate the flesh of swallows and it hated iron. Its voice was said to be like the jingling of copper pans and it could not hear.

Surprisingly, in the early descriptions of the dragon there was no mention of size. However, the storytellers compensated for this omission. It was said that the dragon could change its size at will: it could become the size of a silkworm or could swell to fill the space between heaven and earth. And, apparently, all dragons could rise up until they mounted the clouds and could descend until they were hidden in the fountains of the deep. It also seems that they could make themselves visible or invisible at their pleasure. Some believed that there was a principal all-highest dragon that was the primary image of creation.

By 300 BC dragons were believed to preside over the seasons and divisions of the world: in the east was the Green Dragon, also known as *shen long* or spirit dragon, which was identified with the spring (Fig. 2.1); the White Dragon ruled the west and was identified with autumn; the Black Dragon ruled the north and was associated with winter; and in the south there were two dragons, the Red Dragon and the Yellow Dragon, who divided the duty of ruling the summer. These ancient allocations were officially sanctioned in 1110 during the Song dynasty when these dragons were aggrandized by the granting of princely titles.

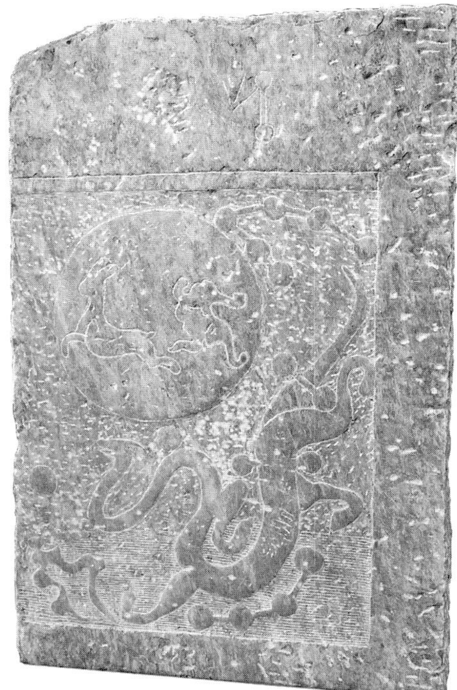

2.1 The Green Dragon, originally the name given to a constellation, was considered the Dragon of the East. This recently unearthed ancient slab depicting the constellation of sixteen stars is believed to date from 55 BC and is now on display at the Ancient Observatory in Beijing.

Chinese dragons were originally considered to be benevolent creatures, benign and not aggressive, although some dragons were known to be ill tempered. There were accounts of tiresome flood dragons that had to be tamed, while the Buddhists, through their tales of the Serpent Kings, introduced into folklore wicked dragons that were unquestionably bad (Fig. 2.2). Legends arose of dragons that needed to be taught a lesson, including one about a savage serpent-like dragon ravaging the countryside, accompanied by a fierce tortoise (of all things), and these beasts having to be slain by a Black Warrior.

Dragons have long been associated with dogs (Fig. 2.3). There is an ancient Chinese saying that 'a brown dog sprouts horns and becomes a yellow dragon'. One story that became popular during the Three Kingdoms period (220–280) was about a young boy, Pan Hu, who grew from a small cocoon found in an old woman's ear into a dog-dragon covered in glossy fur. There is another story of the same period about a man called Lu Junchang who saw two white dogs with elongated bodies and broad chests frolicking about the fields as if floating on a cloud. They dived into a pool and soon after this out flew two dragons, leaving a raging storm in their wake. Lu realized that the two dogs were actually dragons.

There were also dragons with human faces. Were they human-dragons? And there was a creature with the head of a dragon but a human body believed by some to be the Dragon King. Is this a dragon-human? The *Mountain and Water Classic* also refers to a dragon beast with a serpent's body and a human face with red staring eyes. This is considered to be the spirit of the Zhang Wei mountain, also known as the candle dragon.

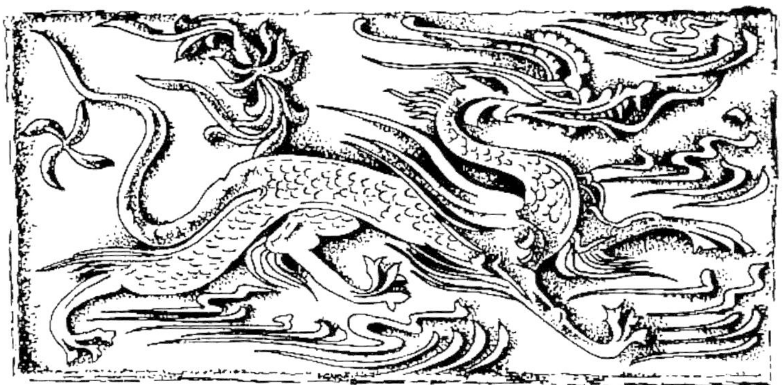

2.2 This Chinese dragon, from a rubbing of an ancient tomb slab dated to the Northern dynasties, is reminiscent of the conventional European dragon. It looks evil, and appears to have wings.

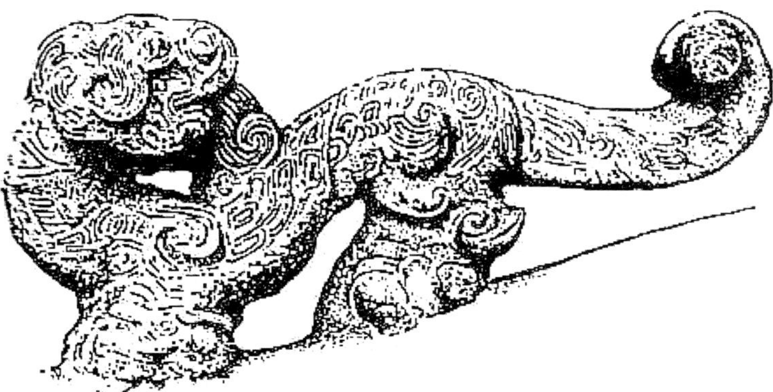

2.3 Ancient bronze vessels had some peculiar animals on them. This dragon, resembling a dog, was used as one of the handles of a bronze vessel dated to the Warring States period.

The common people believed that a dragon could move clouds around and bring rain. This belief was reinforced by the observation that the appearance of a dragon, of which there were many, was usually accompanied or followed by a great downpour. The book *Comments by Zuo* (*Zuozhuan*),[1] a commentary on the *Spring and Autumn Annals* (*Chunqiu*) of Confucius, records an appearance of dragons in the nineteenth year of the Zhaogong emperor, 523 BC, and states that in the Zheng area there was a flood. It goes on to say, 'The dragons were fighting in the deep pools of the Wei River outside the Shi Gate. The people of the country asked the ruler to make sacrifices to the dragons. The emperor refused, saying, "When I fight, the dragons do not interview me. Why should I be the one to interview the dragons when they fight? If I have nothing to ask of the dragons, they will have nothing to ask of me."' A more pragmatic answer you cannot get.

There have been many recorded appearances of dragons in the Fujian area, and these were almost invariably followed by periods of rain. One of the earliest of these appearances took place in the year 540. The Qing-dynasty *History of Fujian* (*Fujian Tongzhi*), volume 271, says 'In the sixth year of the reign of the Dadong emperor, nine dragons gambolled in the morning in the West River at Changzhou.' It also reveals that in 1528 'at Shouning the dragon appeared and there was a great hail storm'.

Incidentally, dragons have also appeared relatively recently. *Nagel's Encyclopaedia Guide* reveals on page 171 that in 1920 a teacher claimed he saw a baby dragon that had fallen from the sky. It stayed, he said, for twenty-four hours, and it had four feet, a cow's head, and a scaly body. What is more, it was 15 metres long and it was blue! It is not recorded whether it rained afterwards.

In times of drought, the people made clay images of the dragon that they sacrificed to for the purposes of making rain. Writer-scholar Wang Chong, who died around AD 90 and was one of the most original and independent thinkers of the Han period (206 BC–AD 220), tells us that a priest who lived around 140–87 BC did just that. The *Masters of the Kingdom of Huainan* (*Huainanzi*), written by several prominent Daoist philosophers around 100 BC, also mentions that 'the clay dragon regulates rain.' Sacrificing to a clay dragon to invoke rain is further noted in the records of the Eastern Han (25–220). In the time of the Tang (618–907) and Song (960–1279) dynasties there was a custom during a severe drought to throw a slab of stone engraved with special invocations into a river or lake in the hope that there would be a favourable response of rain from the dragon residing there. Invocations to the dragon for rain occurred for many centuries. During the Qing dynasty (1644–1911), if there was a severe drought in the Beijing area, it was customary to throw a piece of iron into the Pool of the Black Dragon. This was connected to the ancient Chinese philosophy of the five elements, which asserts that wood produces fire, fire produces earth, earth produces metal, metal produces water, water produces wood, wood produces fire, and so on in an unending cycle. The iron was intended to frighten the Black Dragon for dragons were thought to be afraid of iron. And like a spur to a horse or a jab to an ox, this was intended to serve as encouragement to get on with the task of making rain.

The belief in the power of dragons to make rain persisted and images of the Dragon King for the purpose of invoking rain to end a drought continued throughout the centuries. These images were sometimes made of bamboo, covered with yellow paper or cloth. In his book, *Social Life of the Chinese*, Revd Doolittle describes the ceremony in some detail:

'The head and face are made to imitate the head and face of a dragon; the body and hands are like the body and hands of a man. No feet are attached to it. Being very light it is carried in procession by a man or boy, who places the image over him, the dress coming down to his ankles—in other words, the carrier gets into it. The head of the image is 2 to 3 metres from the ground. In its hands, carried in front of the breast, is a kind of wand, in imitation of the utensil which the courtiers of the Ming dynasty were required to hold before them in the presence of the emperor.' He goes on to say that there were also cloth flags, in yellow, green, black, and white, fastened to bamboo poles and that on each was a prayer offered for rain. The men or boys who carried these flags cried out loud, 'Let it rain!' and 'The rain is coming!' A man carrying two buckets of water would dip a green branch of bamboo and sprinkle water on the ground, calling out while he did so, 'The rain comes, the rain comes!' The procession would often make its way to the magistrate's house, where he would emerge to bow and offer incense to the statue of the Dragon King.

But not all the images were so simply made. On 23 August 1913, prayers for rain to end a severe drought were offered at the Gushan Monastery near Fuzhou, Fujian province. Outside the Monastery's Hall of Guanyin, a table was placed on which rested a gilded bronze image of the Dragon King about half a metre high, bearing the characters, 'The adorable Great Dragon, Lord Buddha of the Five Lakes and Four Seas, who produces rain.' A lengthy ceremony followed, which included the sprinkling of water on the image's head to imitate rain and to provide a hint to the Dragon King as to what was expected of him.

Rain processions were held in many parts of China, usually in the fifth moon,[2] considered to be the birthday of the dragon.

Sometimes the processions were held towards the end of the sixth moon when the rains had broken. In both cases, a long articulated paper effigy of a dragon was paraded through the streets with a dozen men acting as living vertebrae under a cloth painted to look like scales. Gongs were clanged, firecrackers were noisily exploded, and bonfires of paper money were lit. The beast would be illuminated by lanterns, and the burned-out ends of the candles inside that dropped out were eagerly sought by women believing them to be talismans for fertility. This ceremony is perpetuated today as the Lion Dance for the entertainment of tourists.

The association between dragons and water has carried over into the present day. Even at the beginning of the third millennium AD, a water tap or faucet in Chinese is called a 'dragon's head', a water pump is called a 'water-drawing dragon's head', and fire hoses are called 'water dragons'.

Early descriptions of the dragon omitted reference to female dragons—it was assumed at the time that all dragons were male as a matter of course. This meant that if it were necessary to make a present to a dragon to persuade it to do something, like making rain to end a drought, or to persuade it to desist from some displeasing activity, like causing floods, naturally the wise men said to themselves, 'What gift would please me most if I were a dragon?' Sadly the decision was nubile young virginal girls—there are records of young maidens being thrown into lakes or drowned in the sea as a bribe to influence lordly male dragons. But female dragons had to exist for procreation, and later legends declared that they laid their eggs on hillsides, usually near water. The incubation, it was asserted, took 1,000 years. When the eggs hatched, water ran out and the young emerged in the form of small water snakes or lizards. This gave rise to a belief that a water snake was a young dragon, and therefore divine, and it sometimes received honours accordingly. At the birth of their offspring the parents cried out; the cry of the male made the wind rise, while the cry of the female made the wind calm. This conflict had a tendency to cause disarray in local climactic conditions, usually resulting in thunder and lightning, darkness, and torrential rain.

It was asserted that after 500 years the simple dragon changed into a *jiao*, known as the scaly dragon or the flood dragon. After 1,000 years it became a proper dragon, the *long* dragon. A further 500 years had to pass before it turned into a *qi long*, a horned dragon, and a further 1,000 years to become a *ying long*, a winged dragon.

The dragon, in all his variations, initially belonged to the people, and was not specifically or exclusively imperial. However, myths connecting emperors and dragons arose. Liubang (206–195 BC), the first emperor of the Western Han dynasty (206 BC–AD 8), was said to be the 'seed' of the dragon because of the story that his mother had borne him after a dream that she had been impregnated by a dragon. However, association with dragons was not the exclusive prerogative of an emperor and such stories were often applied to anyone who achieved greatness or fame. The populace still retained an awe of dragons as powerful spirits entitled to obedience from everyone and even to worship.

During the Song dynasty there was a significant change in the dragon's status. Emperors now took it as their special emblem and everything relating to imperial use—including clothing, banners and hangings, architectural decor, furnishings, and vessels—began to incorporate the dragon design. This change probably stemmed from the belief that dragons had the power to rise from earth to heaven, something mere mortals could not do. Song-dynasty sovereigns felt that they were like dragons in this respect

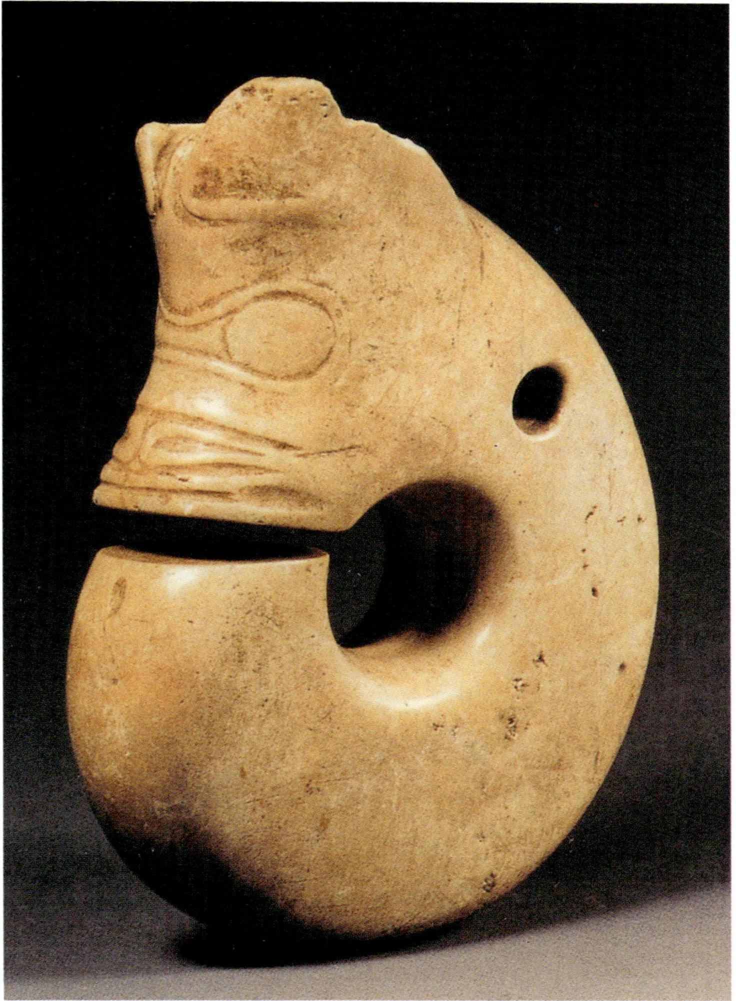

1. In Neolithic times, talismans were used to provide protection from evil or to ensure good luck. It is thought that these pig-faced beasts are forerunners to the dragon, though they bear little resemblance to the shape of the dragon as we know it today.

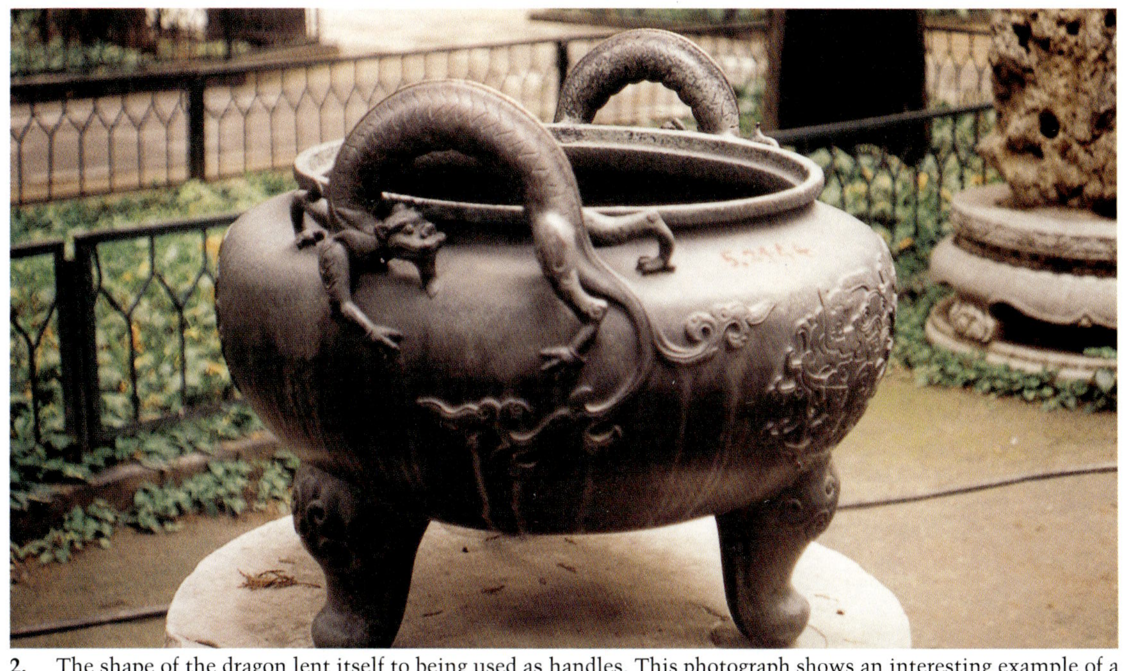

2. The shape of the dragon lent itself to being used as handles. This photograph shows an interesting example of a young four-clawed dragon used as a handle on a bronze bowl, probably Yuan dynasty, at the Temple to Confucius in Beijing.

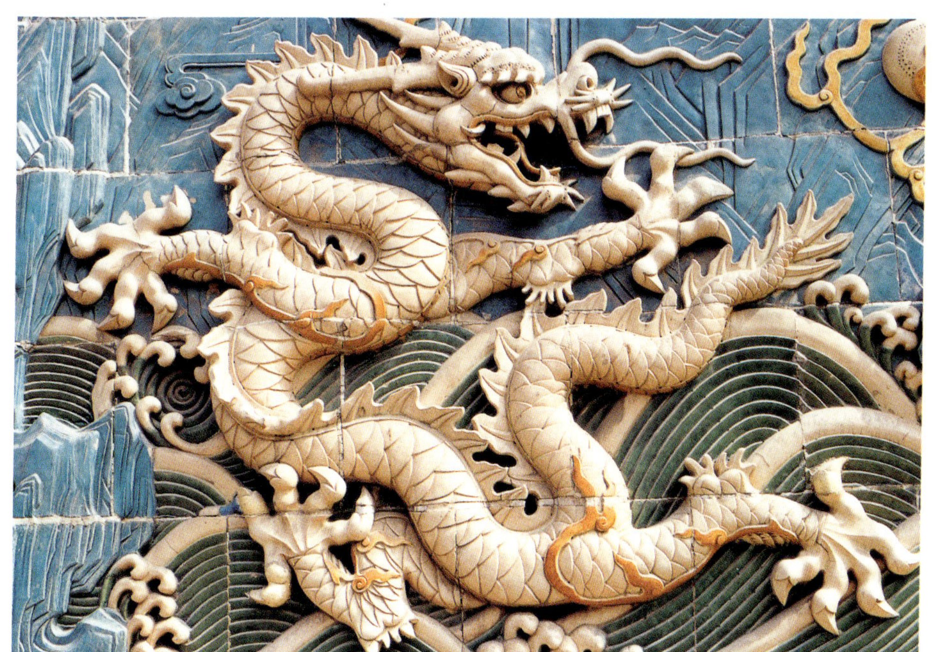

3. The first Ming emperor, determined to eliminate anything from the previous Yuan dynasty, developed the five-clawed dragon and adopted it as his personal emblem, a practice that continued into the next dynasty. This magnificent example is from the Nine-Dragon Screen in the Forbidden City, erected during the early Qing dynasty.

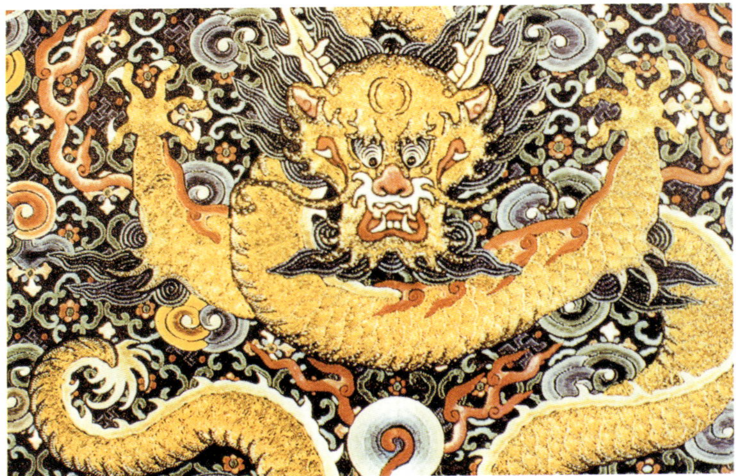

4. The first Ming emperor introduced strict edicts about the design of the dragon and insisted that the five-clawed dragon be used on his robes to indicate his superiority. This dragon, couched in gold thread on a woven ground, is a Qing design based on the Ming modifications.

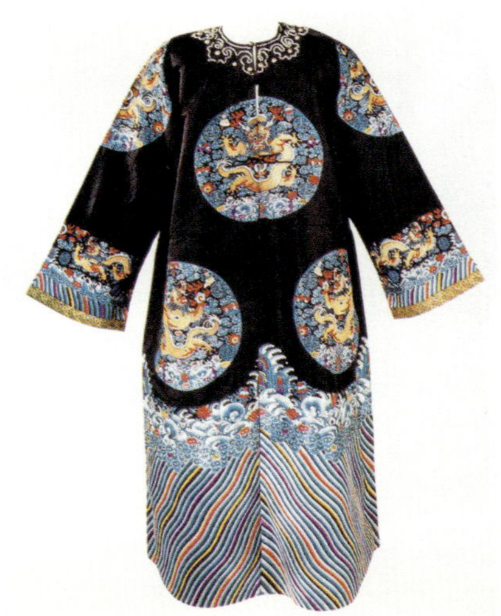

5. A dragon robe for an empress of the early Qing dynasty embroidered with nine dragon medallions, of which eight are visible, but to make up the auspicious number nine a small dragon was embroidered inside the neck opening.

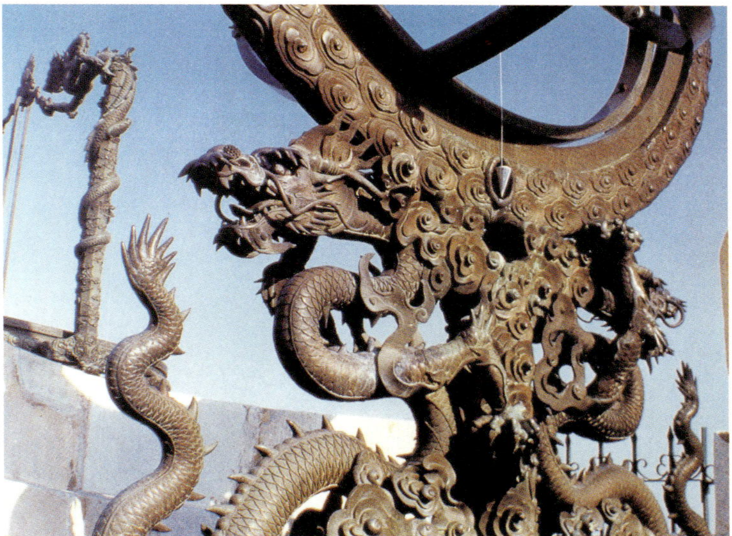

6. The ancient skill of bronze-casting is magnificently displayed in the supports to the astronomical instruments erected during the early Qing dynasty. This breathtaking example was cast during the Qianlong emperor's reign in the late 1700s.

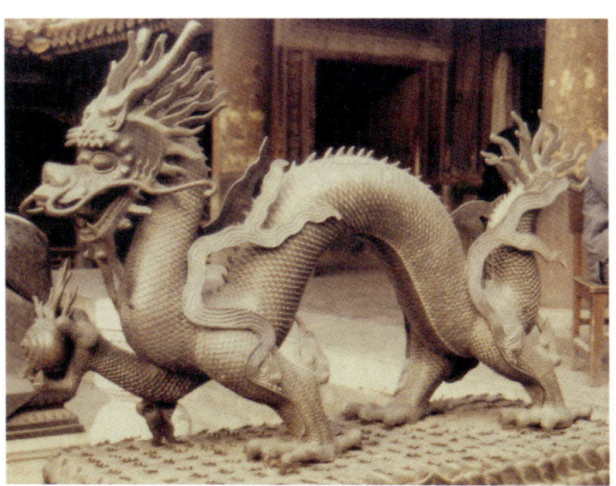

7. The epitome of a dragon is shown in this magnificent example of the bronze-caster's art. It was made for the fiftieth birthday celebrations of the Empress Dowager Cixi in 1884 and is displayed in front of the Palace of Accumulated Elegance in the Forbidden City.

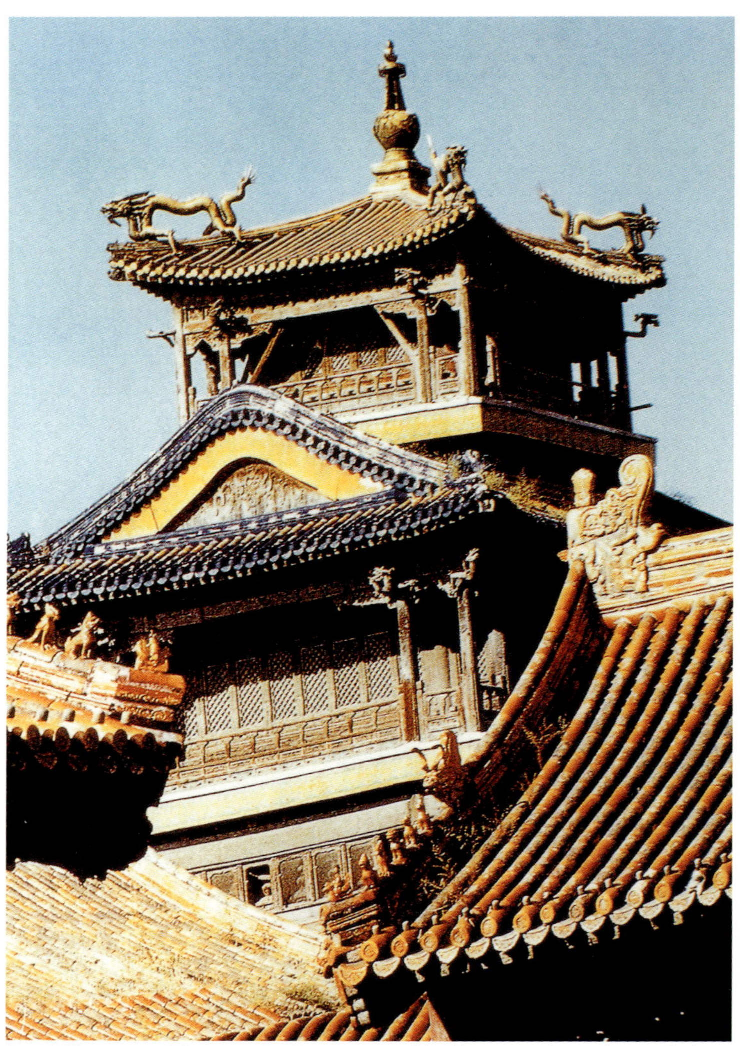

8. Tibetan Buddhist–style dragons in gilded bronze adorn the roof of the Pavilion of Rain Flowers in the Forbidden City. It was built during the Qianlong emperor's reign largely for political reasons.

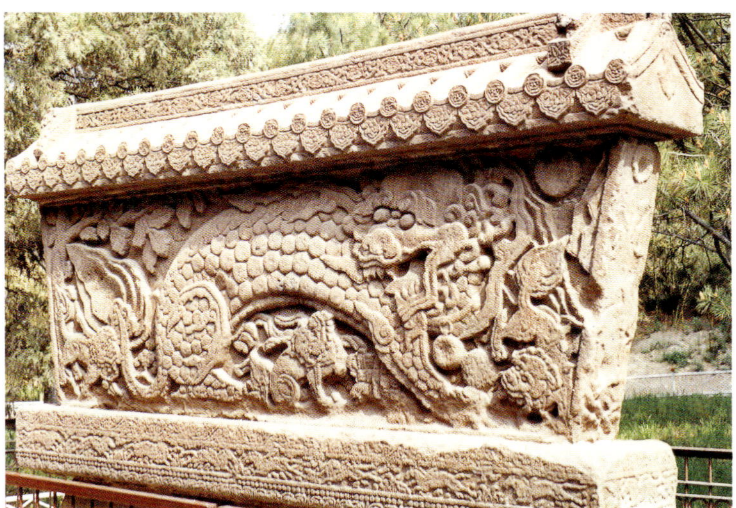

9. This so-called Iron Shadow Screen, now in Beihai Park, is not made of iron—its colouring is part of the natural stone used. It was erected to represent and honour two good dragons who had helped protect the city of Beijing against two evil spirits during the Yuan dynasty.

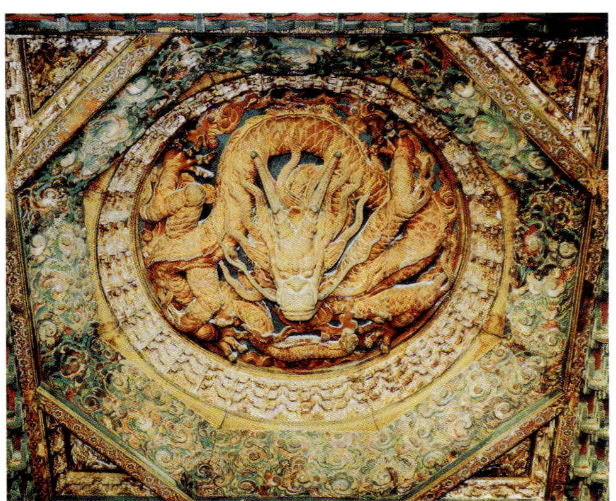

10. This fierce-looking dragon stares down from the caisson ceiling of the Hall of Southern Fragrance. It is one of the few examples in the Forbidden City where the dragon is not concealed by a large ball representing a pearl.

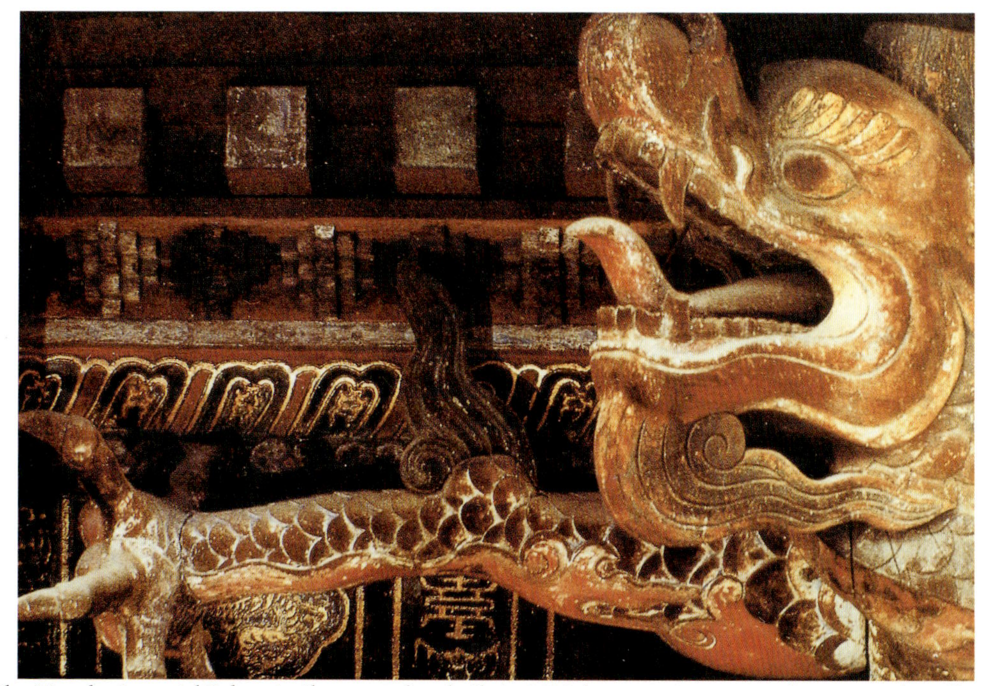

11. The Manchu Imperial Palace in Shenyang, first built in 1625, has some interesting dragons on the pillars at the entrance to Dazheng Hall.

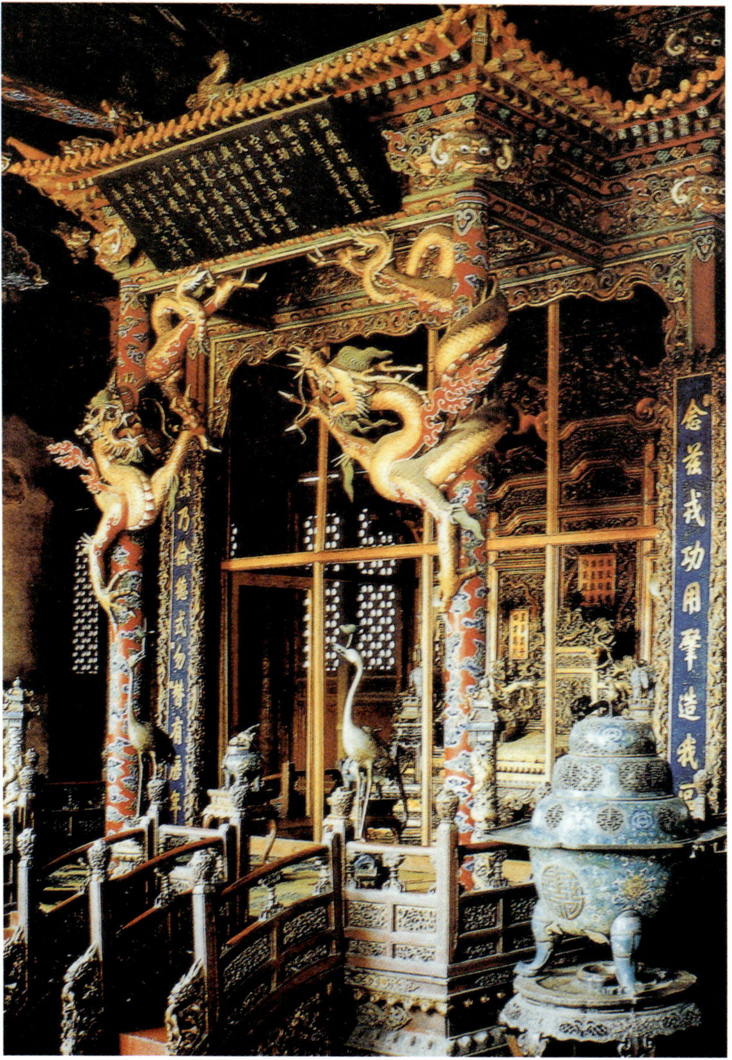

12. The shrine housing the imperial throne in the Manchu Imperial Palace in Shenyang has some magnificent dragons coiled around its pillars.

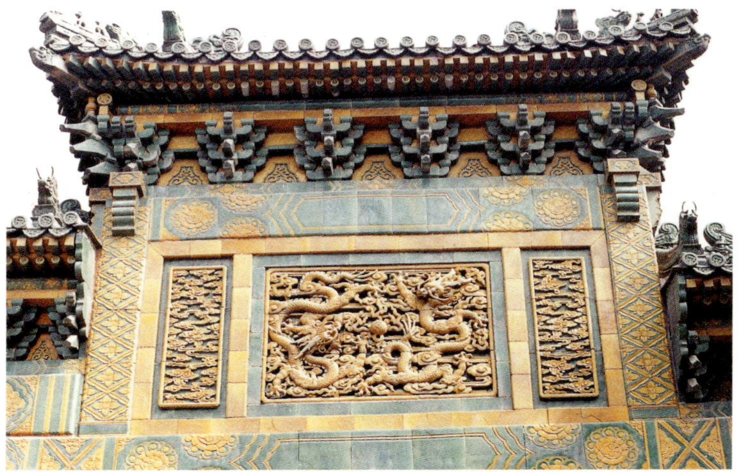

13. The Chinese skill at ceramics is world-famous and, as well as purpose-built dragon screens, examples of glazed dragon panels can be found on decorative gates at many imperial buildings. This splendid example was built in front of a temple in Beihai Park erected for the Qianlong emperor.

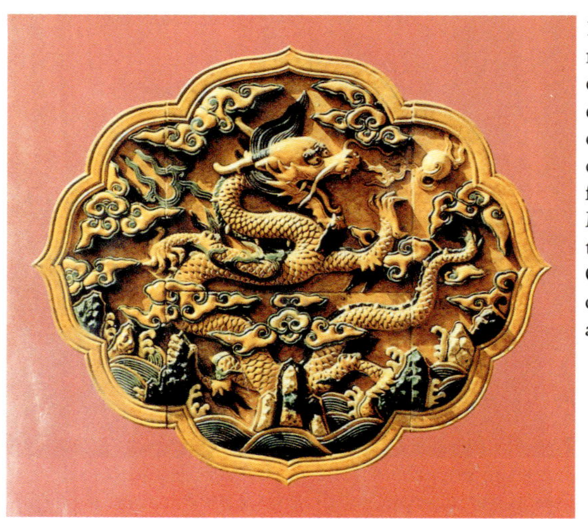

14. There are many dazzling examples of ceramic panels displaying dragons to be found at the Ming Tombs and the Forbidden City, home of this superb ascending dragon.

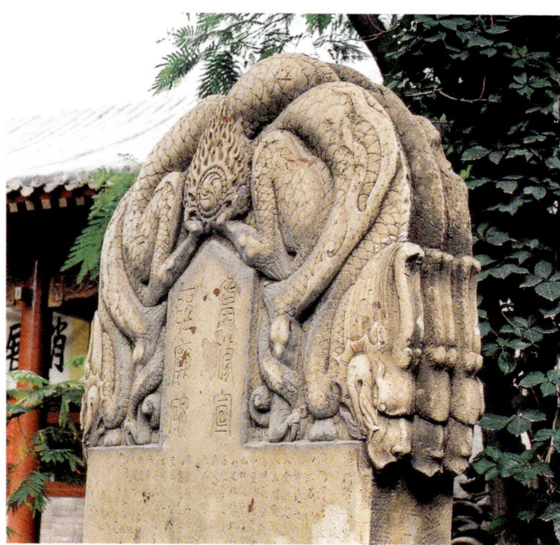

15. The *bixi* is usually depicted side-by-side with another, each looking outward, and often with four dragons entwined together. This stele shows a rare arrangement of six dragons, three looking one way, three the other.

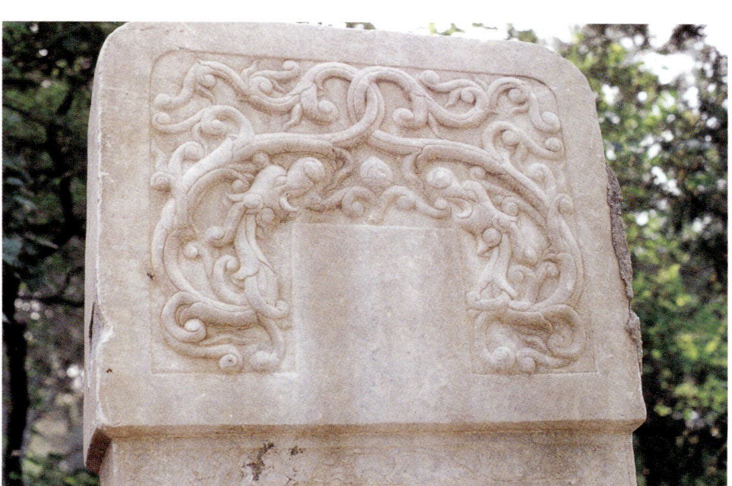

16. The *bixi*, one of the many sons of the dragon, is said to be fond of literature. It is usually carved in pairs. This example is unusual because the heads are looking inwards.

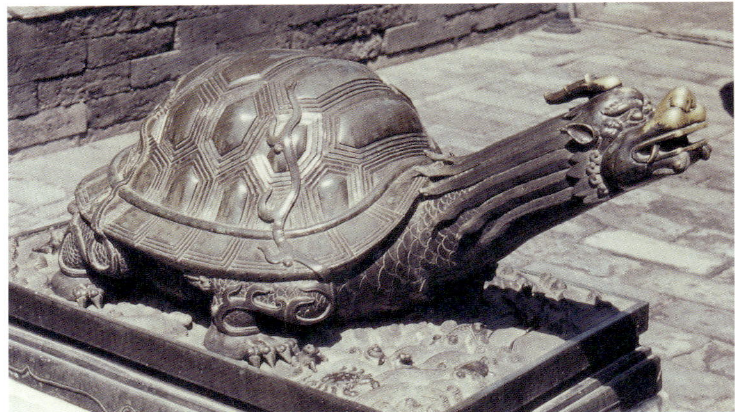

17. This bronze casting of a turtle shows how the head of the beast was significantly changed during Qing times from that of a simple turtle to that of a dragon, making this beast a *baxia*, one of the sons of the dragon.

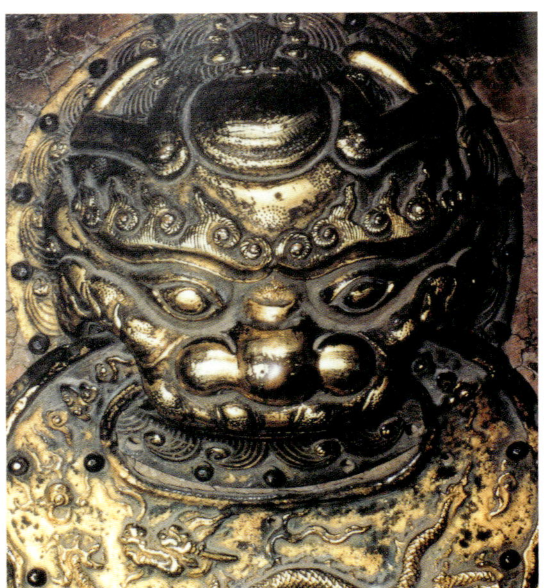

18. Another son of the dragon is the *jiaotu*. He is said to like to close things, and this is the reason he was used as a decorative motif on doors.

19. The *suanni*, a son of the dragon, whose face is carved here on the leg of an incense burner, is said to be fond of smoke.

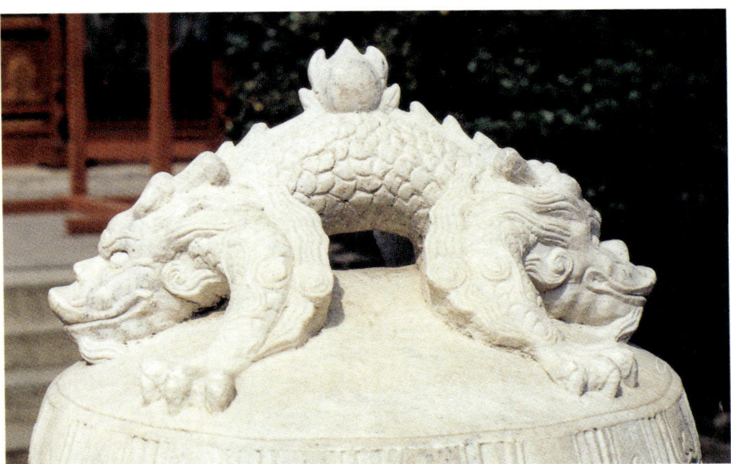

20. Bells in ancient China have long utilized the *pulao*, one of the sons of the dragon, for the handle. In some cases, two dragons were used. In other cases, the dragon is rather like a Siamese twin, as shown here.

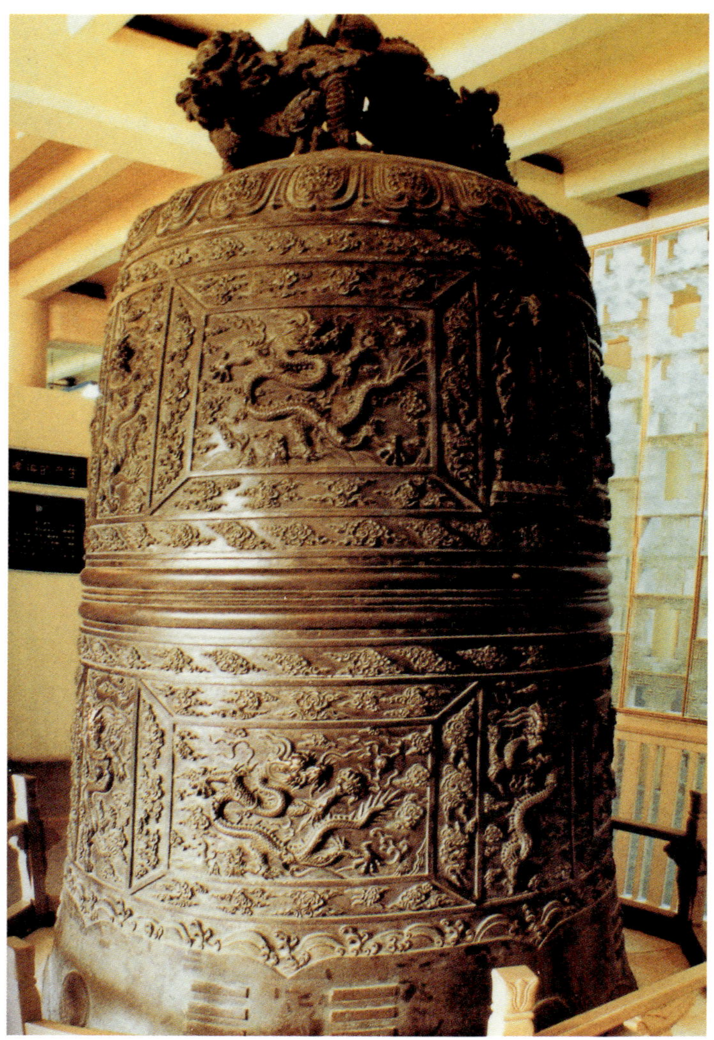

21. There are twenty-two beautiful dragons on this magnificent bronze bell in the Big Bell Temple in Beijing, believed to have been cast for the Qianlong emperor. The detail is breathtaking.

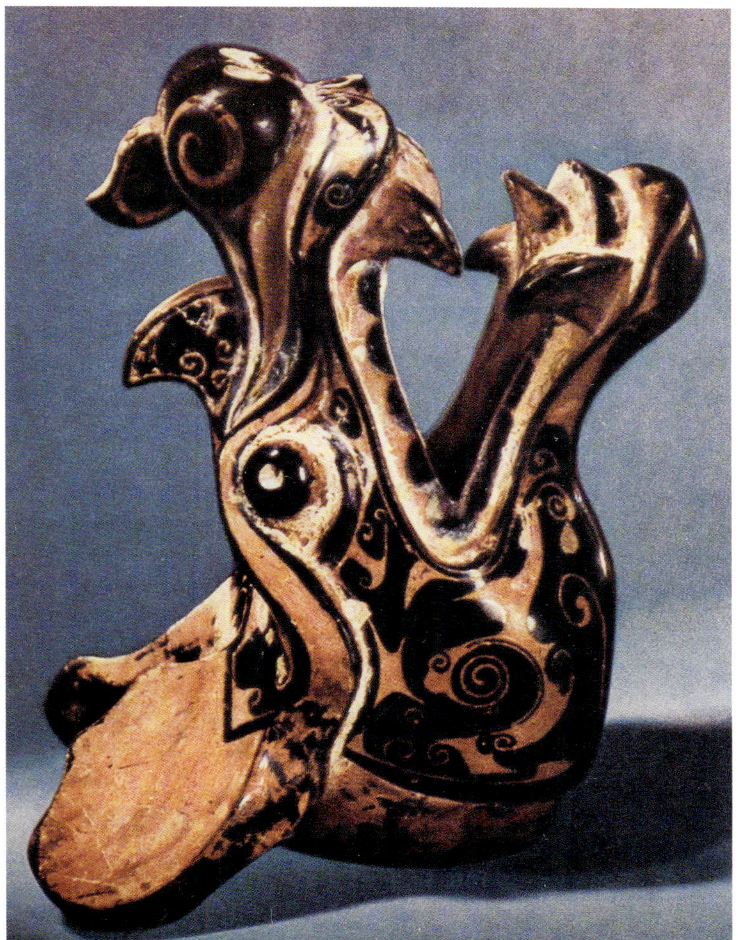

22. Dragon heads were often placed on ornamental staffs for ceremonial purposes, as this fine example shows. Several similar designs have been found. This one dates to the third or fourth century.

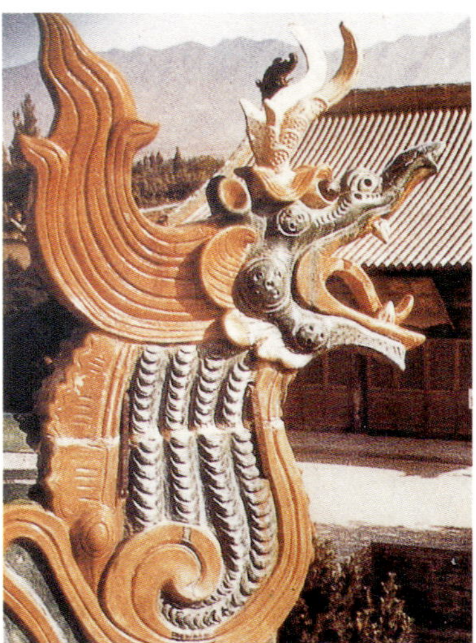

23. This splendidly impressive beast adorns the roof of the Manchu Imperial Palace in Shenyang.

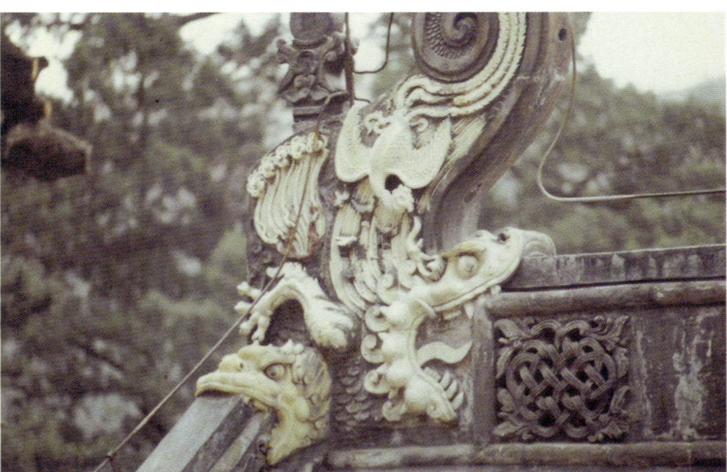

24. The *da wen*, one form of the dragon, is almost invariably found on the roof ridges of important imperial buildings. This one at the Ordination Terrace Temple, near Beijing, is considerably superior in quality to those found on the major halls and palaces in the Forbidden City.

and could therefore legitimately take the dragon as their personal symbol. The word dragon was now used in the name of everything to do with the emperor's life and position. The emperor himself became known as the 'True Dragon' and his person was styled the 'Dragon's Body' or the 'Dragon's Person'. The throne of all emperors was referred to as the 'Dragon's Seat'. Imperial children became the 'Dragon's Seed'. The future emperor was the 'Hidden Dragon'. The imperial way became known as the 'Dragon's Path' or 'Dragon's Way' (Fig. 2.4). The emperor's pen was the 'Dragon's Brush' and the tablet that represented the sovereign in every temple was called the 'Dragon's Tablet'. When he died he was said

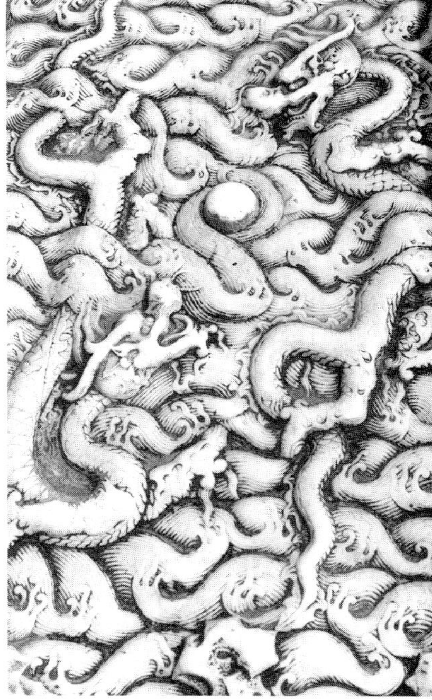

2.4 Many of the stone slabs in the centre of stairways of imperial buildings are carved with dragons. They are known as the 'Dragon's Way', and only the emperor was allowed to be carried over them.

to have 'Mounted the Dragon Chariot' or was now 'Riding the Six-Dragon Chariot'. This was a mythical chariot drawn by six dragons from which the emperor could rule from heaven. Those who remained to serve the new emperor were said to have 'Clung to the Dragon's Beard'. Gradually the sayings drifted into wider use. A rich and elegant person was referred to as a 'Dragon Prince'. An upcoming man could be described as a 'Rising Dragon'. One who had won power could be referred to as a 'Dragon Flying in the Sky'. A loved man was known as a 'Golden Dragon'. Exquisite penmanship was said to be executed by means of a 'Pen Moving as a Dragon'. There was a proverb that said, 'The wife depends on her husband, and the man relies on the dragon: everyone has something to rely on.' Clearly, the dragon remained part and parcel of everyday life, and was not the exclusive prerogative of the emperor.

There are many legends concerning dragons being ridden. One describes how the legendary Yellow Emperor, Huangdi, was once visited by a glittering gold dragon during a lively celebration of a victory over Chi You.[3] He jumped on its back, but while he was astride it his ministers and his concubines followed him. Over seventy people climbed on the dragon. Lower-ranking officials rushed in and grabbed the dragon by the beard and their combined weight was so great that the beard was pulled off. The people howled with dismay. Huangdi's bow was also attached to the beard and so it was named the *wuhao*, the howling weapon. The dragon's beard turned into a flower, the *longxucao*, the Chinese alpine rush (*Eulaliopsis binata*). Not surprisingly the dragon, with such a load, had difficulty in rising to heaven.

Another legend relates the story of Jiu Long, a Buddhist mythical figure with the strength of nine dragons, who pinned the tails of nine wicked dragons to the bed of a lake. The dragons screamed for mercy, so he mounted one, and with the others in tow, he flew to the Nine Dragon Mountain. Nine beautiful girls welcomed him and he was so pleased that he invited his eight brothers to join him and they each married one of these beauties. They have lived in the Nine Dragon Mountain ever since.

Since the dragon was able to fly, would not the heavenly spirits use this beast to ride on? Of course. In a tomb dated to a period between 220 and 580, pottery figures have been found depicting female immortals riding on the symbolic animals of the four cardinal directions, one of which was the Green Dragon. Wall paintings in tombs dated to the Northern dynasties (386–588) depict male immortals riding on dragons. Similar paintings, but in more detail, have been found in tombs of the Tang dynasty, probably influenced by Buddhist stories (Fig. 2.5).

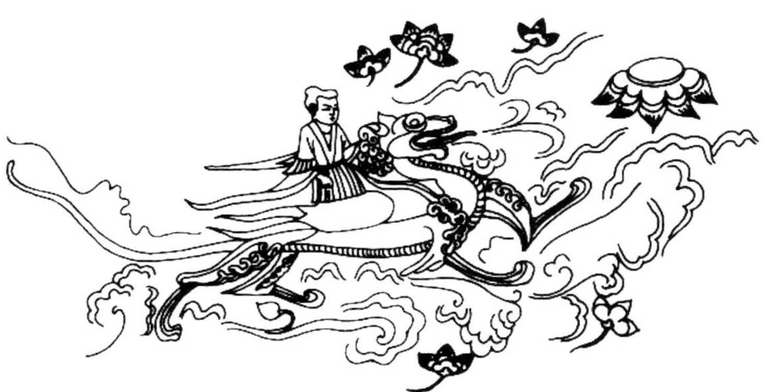

2.5 Tang-dynasty painting of a female immortal riding on a dragon, surrounded by lotus flowers.

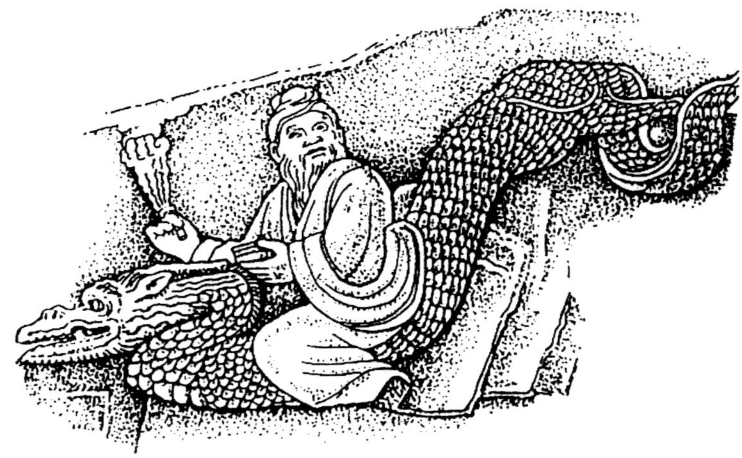

2.6 The Rain Master, Yushi, astride a dragon, as depicted on a Song-dynasty stone carving.

The belief that the Rain Master flew about his business on a dragon was prevalent during the Song dynasty, and a stone carving depicting this has been found (Fig. 2.6).

There is a legend that in ancient times the State of Guizi (now Kuqa in Xinjiang) was terrorized by a vicious dragon with the head of a tiger. The king, a brave soldier, subdued it and rode it back to assure his frightened people. From then on, he always used this dragon as his mount.

The legends referred to so far are Buddhist influenced, but the Daoists had their legends too. Dong Tianci was a famous legendary dragon tamer who assumed the robes of a Daoist priest to overcome a fierce Black Dragon. The dragon was thenceforth made to be his mount.

In other words, the immortals and legendary beings, as well as the emperors and the common people, found the dragon to be a useful beast. The dragon was clearly a true spirit of China.

Notes

1 *Comments by Zuo* was once believed to have been written by Zuo, an ancient historian about whom virtually nothing is known (his last name may have been Qiuming). This classic Confucian text is now believed to have been compiled by an anonymous author during the early part of the Warring States period (475–221 BC).

2 The traditional Chinese calendar is based on a lunar year, the first month of which usually begins on the second new moon after the winter solstice. The fifth moon therefore corresponds approximately to June.

3 Chi You, also known as Qu Rong, is a mythical figure, credited with being the first great rebel. He was defeated after a fierce battle by a general who then took the throne as Huangdi, the Yellow Emperor. Chi You later became one of his ministers, and eventually took the title of Red Emperor and became the God of Fire.

3
The Dragon and Robes

THE SUBJECT OF dragons as they were depicted on robes and costume is covered thoroughly in another book in the Images of Asia series, *Chinese Dragon Robes* by Valery M. Garrett. However, some brief notes are appropriate here.

Ostensibly, an emperor distinguished himself from other men by means of his robes. Curiously, however, the emperors of the Ming (1368–1644) and Qing (1644–1911) dynasties permitted their nobles, senior officials, and even eunuchs to wear costumes that differed only in detail from the imperial costume. Thus it is difficult for the lay observer to differentiate between them. It would also seem that the Chinese themselves had difficulty, for on several occasions it was necessary to issue edicts governing the design and symbolism of costume—yet many a noble ignored these edicts. For example, the emperor and his immediate family were supposed to have the exclusive prerogative of wearing five-clawed dragons, though the emperor sometimes bestowed this honour on his favourites. Princes and lower ranks were expected to restrict themselves to wearing the four-clawed dragon, the *mang*, but this rule was progressively ignored and gradually the five-clawed dragon became universal. It became unthinkable to be seen wearing a four-clawed dragon.

The use by rulers and senior officials of robes decorated with the design of dragons was first recorded in the Tang dynasty (618–907) and then again during the Song (960–1279). It was the Mongols of the Yuan dynasty (1279–1368), however, who established the wearing of what became known as dragon robes, and these had four-clawed *mang* dragons embroidered on them. Once the Ming came to power there was a deliberate reaction against Mongol influences by the first of these emperors, for in his eyes the Mongols were foreigners (i.e. non-Chinese). He therefore instigated the use of five-clawed dragons on his robes to indicate his superiority (Plate 4).

The Ming dynasty is usually considered to be a period of nationalistic and sentimental return to the customs, traditions, and designs of the Tang dynasty, which is often characterized as the golden age of Chinese history. Inevitably artists, designers, and artisans revived the traditional Chinese motifs and continued their names. When the five-clawed *long* dragon was firmly grasped by the first Ming emperor as his imperial symbol, it was broadly as defined by the Han-dynasty scholar-writer Wang Fu (Fig. 3.1). And yet curiously

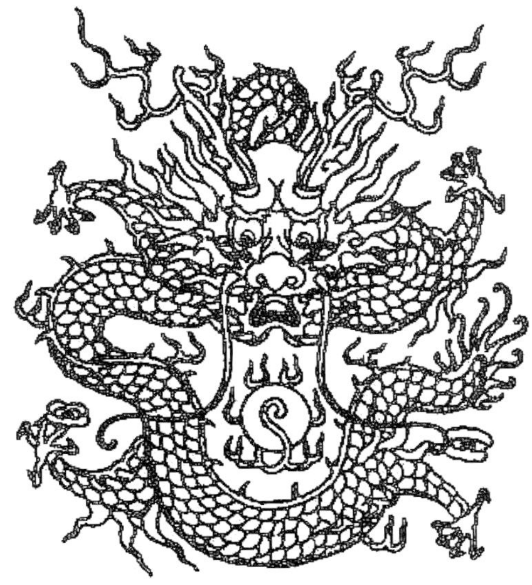

3.1 A classic imperial *long* dragon as most people think of it today, with long serpentine body, four short legs each with five claws, long whiskers at the side of the nose, and a bold direct stare.

in such a conservative environment as the Ming dynasty, subtle innovations and inventions in the design and symbolism of animal motifs were introduced, especially by the Yong Le emperor (1403–1424) and his successors. But was this deliberate, or was it accidental and the result of difficulty in reproducing the elaborate designs accurately? It is possible, of course, that the highly ambitious maritime expeditions initiated by the Yong Le emperor, which reached far across the world and even to Africa, had some influence. The explorers would undoubtedly have brought back descriptions, and perhaps pictures and design motifs, of strange and hitherto unknown beasts.

For formal attire, the emperor wore a robe with a dragon medallion at the front and a dragon square at the back. It had a wide border in a contrasting colour at the edging of the collar and side fastenings. The hem, sleeves, and border were embroidered with no less than 189 dragons, which were intended to clearly establish his lofty rank and to emphasize his incomparable role as the link between heaven and earth. The emperor, and the emperor alone, was allowed to display the full twelve symbols of authority on his robes to demonstrate the virtues and cosmic role of the so-called Son of Heaven. These twelve symbols had been well established over many centuries, first appearing on sacrificial robes in the Zhou dynasty and later during the Han. Indeed, one of these symbols, known as the *fu*, was so ancient that its original meaning had long been forgotten—it became simply a symbol to be used by the emperor alone and symbolized his discernment between good and evil.

The gowns of the emperor were bright yellow except when offering sacrifices to heaven, the sun, or the moon, when he wore blue, red, or white, respectively. There were two dragons for the shoulders, five for the waist, one on the lapel, and another embroidered inside the robe to make up the auspicious number nine. There were also nine dragons each on the front and back panels of the robe. On the skirt, worn under the robe, there were two rampant dragons and four running dragons, while on each sleeve cuff there was one rampant dragon—a plethora of dragons.

Circular medallions were used to indicate rank for the imperial family, with the higher ranks wearing front-facing five-clawed dragons (Plate 5), while the lower ranks wore dragons in profile or the four-clawed dragon. Early Qing-dynasty robes had large, curling snake-like dragons (sometimes called python dragons) on the chest and back, but as the dynasty progressed the upper dragons became smaller and the lower dragons larger until all became the same size.

The robes were designed by artists of the Office of the Imperial Household, approved by the emperor and the Board of Rites, and the designs sent to the weavers. The cloth for these robes was manufactured in special weaving offices, the *zhizao ju*, in the silk industrial cities of Jiangning (near Nanjing), Suzhou, and Hangzhou. Creating a robe could take as much as thirty months. The gold work and the silk embroidery could take a further twelve months on top of that! There was a continuous activity to produce these gowns and robes.

The Ming civil and military officials continued the Yuan-dynasty practice of wearing square embroidered badges on their formal robes to denote their rank. There was much confusion at first, and some of the nobles and officials struck out on new paths of their own. Some designs were quite innovative and gradually it became obvious that something had to be done to curb this initiative—there are records of restrictions imposed by the emperor against the use of some of the unconventional designs. For example, an edict issued by the Tianshun emperor in 1459, just two years after being restored to the throne, expressly forbade the use on badges of rank of military officers of a dragon with wings.

As noted in Chapter 1, winged dragons, known as *ying long*, are mentioned in the Ming encyclopaedia, *Collected Illustrations of the Three Realms*. However, *ying long* were known long before this encyclopaedia was published. In the University Museum in Philadelphia, there is a fine example of a *ying long* with two horns on an embroidered imperial badge of unknown age. It has three claws, although Ming

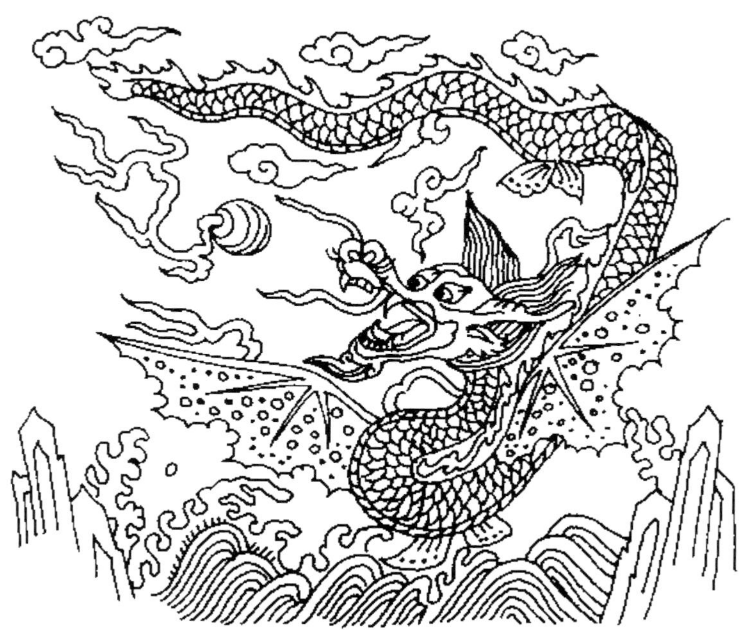

3.2 A robe with the *fei yü* flying fish motif, a dragon with bat-like wings, could be bestowed on favoured ministers of state and other worthy courtiers.

and Qing drawings usually show the *ying long* with five claws. It is not a winged fish with a dragon's head, as has sometimes been suggested, even though winged fish, usually termed *fei yü* (flying fish), were used on robes (Fig. 3.2). The *Ming Dynastic History* (*Ming Shi*) states that eunuchs wore such robes at the beginning of the Yong Le period, but does not reveal whether this had official approval. Neither does it provide an illustration of what a *fei yü* looked like, and unfortunately no designs of robes with *fei yü* patterns have survived. Later references assert that the right to use the *fei yü* flying fish motif was bestowed upon certain ministers of state and worthy courtiers, and in 1510 a robe with a *fei yü* patterned square was given to a Japanese envoy who had come to the Ming court with a tributary gift from the 'King of Japan', Shogun Yoshizumi.

4
Dragons in Art

SCULPTURAL REPRESENTATIONS of dragons are remarkably rare and few large-scale sculptures in stone, clay, or bronze have been found older than the late Qing dynasty (1644–1911). Several small clay figures have been found in various tombs in China and isolated examples exist in museums around the world. Several small gilded bronze models believed to be early dragons have been found in tombs of the Tang dynasty (618–907), especially around Xian. One, 18 centimetres long, was found in a tomb excavated in 1979. The creature has a long slender neck, an open mouth displaying fangs, whiskers, and a curled tongue. It also has a pointed snout, a tuft of hair at the back of its head, and zigzag protuberances along its back. The body is more of the feline type, although it has scales, and it has a long, curled Tang-dynasty style tail. The feet have three claws.

An exquisite pair of dragons made of pure gold, only 4 centimetres in length, was found in a tomb excavated in 1970 at Hejiacun, a suburb of Xian in Shaanxi province. Another even more interesting dragon, much larger at a height of 34 centimetres, has been found in a Tang-dynasty tomb at Caochangpo village, again near Xian. This has only two feet and has an upright sinuous body with two small wings: this is obviously a Tang version of the *kui* dragon.

Some excellent bronze castings of dragons can be seen at the Ancient Observatory in Beijing, the Guanxiangtai. This displays a set of astronomical instruments, most of which were made under the supervision of Father Verbiest, a Jesuit missionary, who was directed to update the observatory by the Kangxi emperor in 1674. The supports for the instruments are breathtaking, being in the shape of imperial dragons (Plate 6). Similar instruments exist in the Purple and Gold Hill Observatory (Zijinshan Tianwentai) in Nanjing, also with magnificent bronze dragons acting as supports. These are of Ming manufacture and were moved there from Beijing in 1933.

In 1884 two superb bronze castings of dragons, each holding a flaming pearl in the five claws of their right feet, were placed in front of the Palace of Accumulated Elegance (Chuxiugong) in Beijing's Forbidden City, now known as the Palace Museum. They were part of the extensive (and expensive) renovations carried out in honour of the Empress Dowager Cixi's fiftieth birthday (Plate 7).

The Forbidden City has four other three-dimensional *long* dragons. They are of gilded bronze and are on the eaves of the Pavilion of Rain Flowers (Yuhuage), a three-storied pavilion built by the Qianlong emperor (1736–1795) for the practice of Lamaism (Plate 8). There are similar *long* dragons to be found on the roof of the Xumifushou Tibetan Temple built for him at the Summer Palace at Chengde in Heibei province in 1780.

Light relief carvings of dragons are more common—one of the earliest examples is to be found on the side of a huge black jade bowl, believed to have been presented to Kublai Khan in 1265, on display in the Round Fort (Tuancheng), outside the southern gate of Beijing's Beihai Park. Marco Polo commented on this bowl, noting that it 'exceeds the value of four towns'.

A large panel of volcanic stone, known as the Tieyingbi or Iron Shadow Screen, carved with a dragon in light relief, is displayed at the northern edge of Beihai Park (Plate 9). Rumour had it that it was impregnated with iron from a smelting works that used to be nearby, but the colour derives from the natural brownish shade of the stone used. It dates from the Yuan dynasty (1279–1368) and formerly stood in Fruit Market Street inside the gate known as Gate of Moral Victory (Deshengmen), but many years before that it had stood outside the gate in front of a temple and was erected to protect the city of Beijing from two evil spirits who had been outwitted by two kind dragons.

The imperial throne in the Hall of Supreme Harmony (Taihedian) in the Forbidden City, and a similar throne in the Manchu Imperial Palace in Shenyang, in Liaoning province, are one mass of dragons; so many in fact that it is hardly possible to detect the individual beasts. Dragons in light relief can be found in both palaces, carved on the balustrades or the sides of bridges.

Caisson ceilings are an old-established feature of Chinese traditional architecture dating back to the Han dynasty (206 BC–AD 220). Known as *caojing* (aquatic plant wells), they opened up the room space and were considered to be protection against fire. The Song-dynasty building regulations, the *Yingzao fashi*, describes two methods of making caisson ceilings. The Ming and Qing dynasties, however, advanced the construction and developed upper, middle, and lower sections. The lower section became a square opening, the middle octagonal, and the highest became circular. Each caisson has a *pan long* (coiled dragon) in the centre (Fig. 4.1). A large ball called a *mingjing* (bright mirror) dangles from the *pan long* in the central span of the caisson. Unhappily, this dangling ball, which represents a pearl, usually conceals much of the dragon from the viewer. Magnificent examples of Ming-designed caissons can be found in the Forbidden City, the one in the Hall of Supreme Harmony, the biggest, being considered the best. Another outstanding example is to be found on the ceiling of the Hall of Southern Fragrance (Nanxundian) (Plate 10).

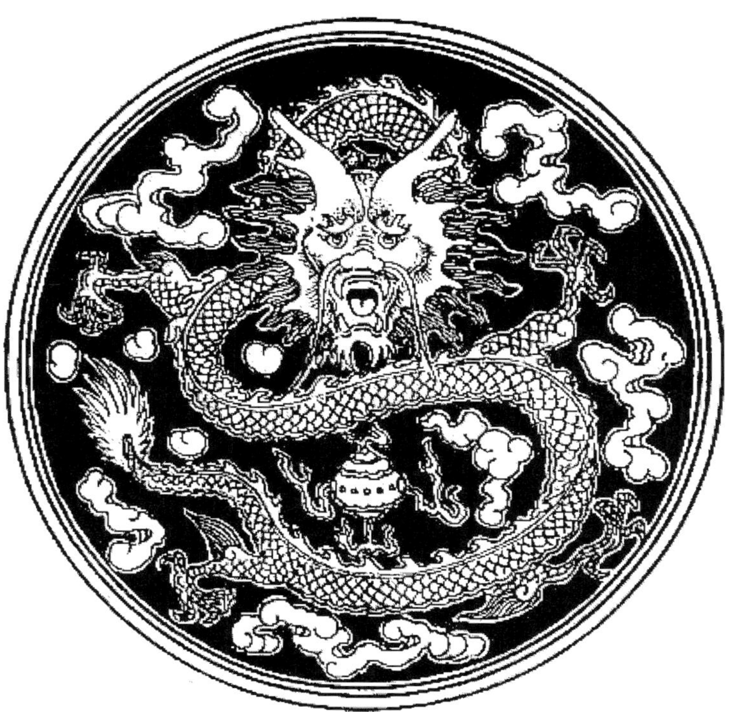

4.1 The *pan long* could cavort in the clouds but was forbidden to ascend to heaven.

The dragon, having a snake-like body, curves naturally and easily around pillars, and there are dragons carved in light relief coiled around the four *hua piao* (glory marks of distinction) on either side of Gate of Heavenly Peace (Tiananmen). Similar designs can be found in gold on the main wooden pillars of the Hall of Supreme Harmony in the Forbidden City. There are also beautiful examples of dragons on pillars at the Dazheng Hall of the Manchu Imperial Palace in Shenyang (Plate 11) and on the shrine housing the imperial throne in the Chongzheng Hall, while cloisonné dragons coil around the tall column-shaped incense burners in front of the throne in the main hall (Plate 12). There are also superb coiling dragons on the stone pillars in the temple dedicated to Confucius at Qufu in Shandong province. This temple was set up only one year after his death, but has been considerably rebuilt, modified, and enlarged over the years. The magnificent stone pillars are probably a Qing-dynasty replacement.

There are three glazed ceramic nine-dragon screens (*jiu long bi*) in China. They were positioned to ward off evil spirits that might adversely affect temples or an exalted imperial residence (Plate 13). The largest is in the city of Datong in Shanxi province, and was erected in 1368 in the first year of the first Ming emperor. The second is in Beijing's Beihai Park, which was erected in 1417 in the Yong Le era. It was placed there to protect the Hall of Ten Thousand Buddhas. Unfortunately, it failed to do so, for the hall burnt down and no longer exists. The screen was probably restored during the Qianlong period, and perhaps also in the past fifteen years or so. The most magnificent nine-dragon screen is in the Forbidden City facing the Gate of Imperial Supremacy (Jidianmen). It was erected in 1771 when the area around the Palace of Tranquil Longevity (Ningshougong) was being rebuilt for the Qianlong emperor to use when he retired after sixty years of reign. The central dragon, a Qing-dynasty style innovation called a sitting dragon, is yellow and stares imperiously at the viewer. On each side are blue, white, black, and yellow dragons rising from rolling waves against a background of clouds swirling around mountains, each staring at a flaming pearl. They are moulded in high relief, the thickest part at their foreheads standing 20 centimetres out from the surface. The dragons in profile, with their heads uppermost, are known as ascending dragons (Plate 14). The dragons with body and tail uppermost are called descending dragons. On the top ridge there are eight dragons running towards a central coiled dragon.

The screen has a delightful story connected to it. When it was completed and ready for inspection by the Qianlong emperor, a piece fell off one of the tiles. There was no time to get a new one, so with commendable initiative the workman in charge had a piece of wood put in its place that had been carved and then painted to look like ceramic. That piece of wood is still there today, and can be seen on the third dragon from the left.

There is also a three-dragon screen in Datong. It was erected in Ming times in front of a Buddhist temple, which is now in ruins. This dragon screen's protective power was, sadly, also ineffective.

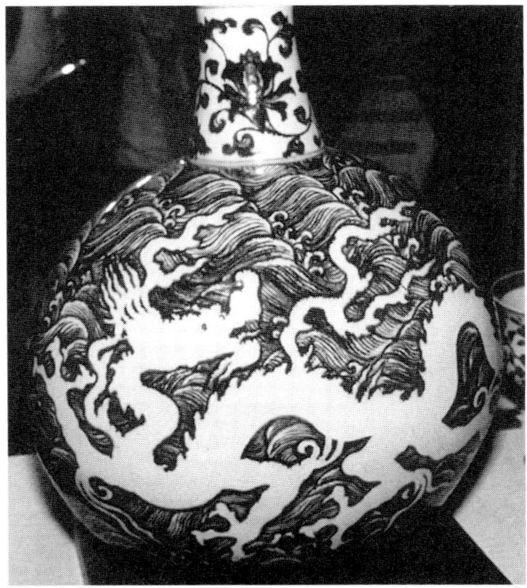

4.2 This three-clawed dragon decorates a Yuan-dynasty vase, on display in the Palace Museum, Beijing.

Paintings showing Chinese dragons are surprisingly rare, but there is a superb example by the Southern Song artist Chen Rong, held at the Museum of Fine Arts, Boston, in the United States. Chen Rong would start his paintings while drunk, dip his cap in ink, and smear the design on paper. He would finish the detail with a brush.

Depictions of dragons abound on ceramics (Fig. 4.2), so much so that an entire book could be devoted to these. Regretfully, considerations of space preclude a discussion of dragons and ceramics in this volume.

5
The Many Sons of the Dragon

THE DRAGON IS usually credited with having nine sons and though they all possess some great talent none of them perfectly resemble their 'father'. Several ancient publications list the characteristics of the nine sons, but unhappily they differ. There are also several lists devised more recently and these differ again. It is clear that the Chinese have not come to any agreement as to who the sons are.

C. A. S. Williams, in his book *Outlines of Chinese Symbolism and Art Motives*, quotes a list given by Chen Renxi (1579–1634) in his book *Encyclopaedia of Hidden and Real Conditions* (*Qianqueju Leishu*). This list names the *chiwen* (not to be confused with *chiwei*, the large beasts on the end of the roof ridges in the Forbidden City, which are sometimes mistakenly referred to as *chiwen*), *pulao*, *bian*, *yazi*, *suanni*, *qiuniu*, *bixi*, and the *chaofeng*. But he also mentions that there are other slightly different lists. One includes the *jiaotu* and the *taotie*, and also a *zhayu*. The inclusion of this last beast, with the suggestion that it is a son of the dragon, is intriguing and will be discussed later.

A chapter in a book entitled *Dragon*, by Wang Congren, which is largely a compilation of legends about the dragon, gives the same list attributed to Chen Renxi by Williams, but says that this list came from a man called Liu Ji. Apparently, the Hongzhi emperor asked his Grand Academician, Li Dongyang (1447–1516), who the nine sons were. Li was unable to answer, but Liu Ji, an official with the Ministry of Personnel, came to Li's rescue and gave his opinion.

Dr Florence Ayscough (1878–1942), a well-known authority on symbolism in Chinese art, in her 1921 article,

Notes on the Symbolism of the Purple Forbidden City, mentions Li Dongyang's list, saying that he himself presented this to the Hongzhi emperor—she makes no mention of Liu Ji. However, the list she attributes to Li names the last four as *jiaotu*, *beixi*, *taotie*, and *baxia*. This list is generally quoted in discussions on the nine sons of the dragon in current tourist publications.

Chen Renxi mentions the *chaofeng* as a son of the dragon, and Williams adds that the *chaofeng* 'is carved on the eaves of temples, owing to its liking for danger', but gives no explanation as to why temple eaves should be associated with danger. Wang Congren says, briefly but more reasonably, that the *chaofeng* was inquisitive and adventurous, and was placed on rooftops to frighten away evil spirits and stave off disaster. He gives a drawing of this beast that is identical with those on the eaves of buildings in the Forbidden City—the roof ridges of all Ming and Qing imperial buildings there are traditionally decorated with a series of small figures, the first of which is always the *chaofeng*. This animal is always referred to as a dragon, but it is clearly not a conventional imperial *long* dragon. It squats, has a short thick neck, and has a short bushy tail. Its body is not serpentine, but it does have scales, claws, and two horns. A drawing on page 71 of Wang Congren's book in the chapter entitled 'Sons of the Dragon' accurately depicts this so-called dragon and refers to it as a *chaofeng*.

It is a mystery why the *chaofeng* should be placed at the forefront of the animals on the eaves instead of a conventional *long* dragon. And why is it followed by a phoenix, if it is a phoenix, for the *chaofeng* and the phoenix have never been associated? If the *chaofeng* is capable of frightening away evil spirits that could cause disasters, this would make it a potentially useful beast to be placed in this prominent position. However, although it is displayed on the roof of every building in the Forbidden City, the frequency of disasters, both natural and man-made, reflects sadly on its alleged powers.

But is it a *chaofeng*? The *Beijing Tourist Magazine* in 1989 agrees with the list given by Chen Renxi but says that the dragon's son who is carved on eaves is a *haoxian*, and this list and this name is repeated in the web page, www.chinapage.com. The *haoxian*, however, is not a dragon; it is a celestial beast with extraordinary powers. One can only conclude that the mystery of this first animal's identity, and the reason for its inclusion, has not yet been solved.

Both Chen Renxi's list, quoted by Williams, and Li Dongyang's list, quoted by Ayscough, say that a dragon's son is to be found on sword blades and that this son is a *yazi*. But no example of a Chinese sword with the head of a dragon on it has been found, although photographs of toy swords are sometimes given in the guidebooks. But is it a *yazi*? Ayscough calls it a *yaichai*, though she gives it the same Chinese character.

So which list is correct, and who drew it up, Li, Liu, or Chen? Did the dragon have more than nine sons? The *Beijing Tourist Magazine* happily admits that even 'the Chinese themselves seem unable to achieve agreement as to what the dragon's sons are called.' Yes, indeed!

The assertion that there are nine sons (and only nine sons) must be taken with a pinch of Chinese spice powder, for it is possible to collect a total of nineteen, all stated by one expert or another to be a son of the dragon. The reality, however, is that the suggestion that there are only nine sons exists simply because nine is an auspicious number. Let us now look at these sons of the dragon in more detail.

Beixi

The *beixi* is said to be fond of gazing and looking outwards. It is also believed to have a fondness for water, and is therefore often placed on bridges or at spots close to water, such as canals. There is a head of a dragon gazing at the water mounted on the bridge in front of the Pavilion of Literary Profundity (Wenyuange), the imperial library in the Forbidden City. There are also two *beixi* gazing at the water at the Pavilion of Auspicious Clarity (Dong Rui Ting) and the Jade Green Floating Pavilion (Fu Bi Ting) (Fig. 5.1). Sometimes the *beixi* is referred to as a *chiwen*, but this is incorrect.

Bixi

This son of the dragon often appears on the top of tombstones and steles and, perhaps for that reason, is sometimes thought of as being bowed down with grief (Plate 15). However, the explanation comes after the reality and the reason for this traditional style of stele top is still a mystery. It is simply a tradition. The *bixi*, who is said to be fond of literature, is often

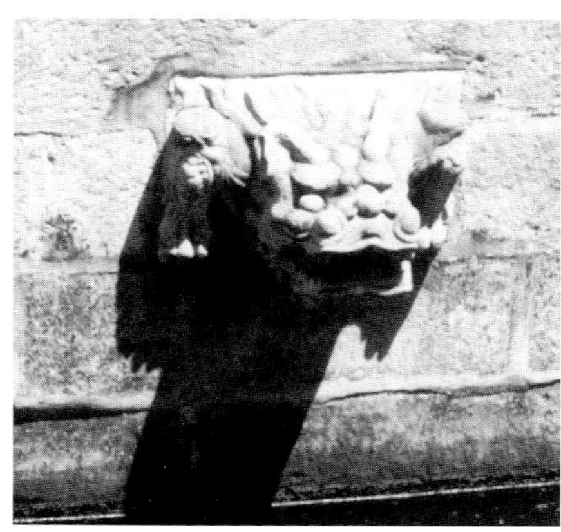

5.1 One of the so-called sons of the dragon, the *beixi* can often be found gazing at water. This one can be seen at the Jade Green Floating Pavilion in the Forbidden City.

carved on the top of stone tablets, invariably in intertwined pairs, each with a head looking outwards, although there are examples of *bixi* looking inwards (Plate 16).

Baxia

The beast carved at the bottom of stone monuments obviously has the capacity to bear heavy weights. Most people assume this is a giant turtle and they are probably right. Certainly in the early days it was a simple turtle, as can be seen in ancient stone carvings that have survived. The concept of it being a mythical beast with a dragon's head is not more than a few hundred years old. This is because the tortoise, or turtle, developed unfortunate connotations because of the shape of its head—it was likened to a penis. Therefore, to call someone a 'turtle head' was a great insult. Turtles and tortoises also developed a bad reputation because people found that it was difficult to differentiate the male and female of the species. Obviously, it was not acceptable to have the tablets at the tombs of highly respected men supported by what were judged to be 'tainted' beasts, especially at the tombs of emperors, so it became necessary to endow the animal with special characteristics: the humble tortoise or turtle had to undergo transmogrification into a dragon. And obviously, if it were a dragon, it had to have a dragon's head (Plate 17). Over the years, the tablet-bearing turtle became a *baxia*, and a son of the dragon in its own right. Unhappily, some writers have mixed up the *baxia* with the *bixi* or the *beixi*.

A magnificent bronze casting of a *baxia*, but without a weight on its back, was used as an incense burner on the front terrace of the Hall of Supreme Harmony. It dates only to the later part of the Qing dynasty (1644–1911).

Jiaotu

There are many gilded decorative plates on the gates in the Forbidden City, and these look rather like door handles, but they are only ornamental masks without specific function. The necessity for an explanation has given vent to the declaration that they are *jiaotu*, the son of the dragon that is said to like to close things (Plate 18). However, it is difficult to see why the figure depicted on these plates should be considered as being a dragon in any form, nor why they are fixed on the palace doors. They are almost certainly nothing more than decoration, for neither a door handle nor a knocker, as they are sometimes referred to, would have any practical use on the huge heavy palace doors.

Suanni

The *suanni* is often carved on Buddha thrones because, it is said, this dragon son has the propensity for resting and contemplating. However, the true reason for this tradition has been long forgotten. The *suanni* has also been identified with the *shizi*, a symbolic lion. *Suanni* are often found carved on the legs of incense burners, again for no clear reason. However, by reverse reasoning, it is said to be fond of smoke and this is why its face is found there. Inside the Imperial Garden (Yuhuayuan) there is a magnificent incense burner that was made in the Qianlong era. It stands near the two huge, fierce-looking bronze beasts called *zhayu*, and is in front of a small gate, portentously called the First Gate in Heaven. The burner was brought from the Summer Palace at Chengde. Each leg has a *suanni* face on it—on incense burners, the *suanni* is a face without a body (Plate 19). However, the term *suanni* is sometimes applied to a leonine beast with scales, yet the animal usually said to be a *suanni* on the Forbidden City roof eaves has no scales.

Taotie

A strange design looking somewhat like a human face is commonly found on ancient bronze food vessels. Tradition has it that this is a *taotie* and that because the beast has a gluttonous nature its face is put on these vessels as a warning to humans to avoid this sin. The *taotie* design can be seen on many of the ancient bronze food vessels on display in the Palace Museum. These vessels are not in any way connected with the Forbidden City, however, and belong to a very much earlier age. Similar bronzes can be seen in many other museums throughout China. The *taotie* design is certainly ancient (Fig. 5.2). Legend has it that Tao Tie was a person who became famous as a glutton during the reign of Yao, the legendary emperor of China's Golden Age, who is said to have ascended the throne nearly two and a half thousand years BC. He abdicated in favour of Shun, who supposedly banished Tao Tie. A common design on ritual bronze vessels and implements of the Shang (*c.*1700–1027 BC) and Western

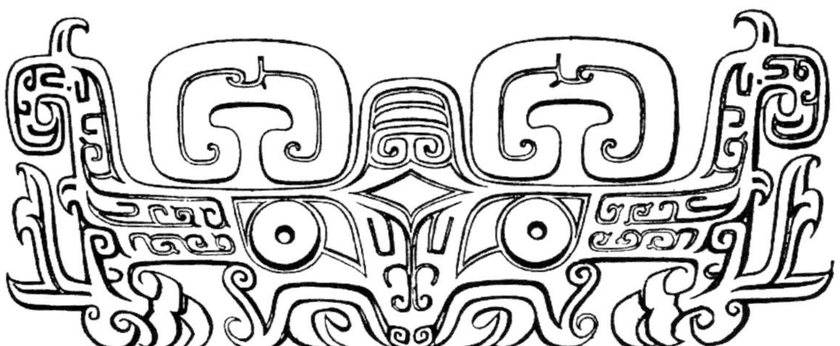

5.2 The ancient *taotie* design was often used on ritual bronze vessels and implements of the Shang dynasty. It characteristically consists of a zoomorphic mask in full face.

Zhou (*c*.1027–771 BC) dynasties is said to be a representation of the face of the person Tao Tie. However, it characteristically consists of a zoomorphic mask in full face that simultaneously may be divided through the centre of the nose ridge to form two profile views of so-called one-legged beasts (*kui* dragons) facing each other. The *taotie* design typically features large, protuberant eyes with stylized depictions of eyebrows, horns, nose crest, and ears. It often has two peripheral legs as well, and a line of a curled upper lip with exposed fangs. However there is no lower jaw, and it is this absence which gives the effect of a wide-open mouth that suggests an infinite capacity for swallowing. Song-dynasty antiquarians explained that the design represented a warning against overindulgence, though whether this was ever a vice in early China is speculation. Since the wide-open mouth design suggests an ever-devouring glutton, it was probably this last feature that later, in the third century BC, led to the name *taotie* for the ancient monster motif. The function of this motif has been variously interpreted. It is possibly totemic or protective, or even an abstracted, symbolic representation of the forces of nature. After the early Zhou period, the *taotie* mask motif was supplanted by another design that was similar but which was depicted more literally and with diminished emphasis.

As with the *jiaotu*, it is not easy to fathom why a conviction developed that the *taotie* design is a son of the dragon. It has never been other than a design on a food vessel, and at the time of its first depiction it is unlikely that it was considered as an idealized portrait of a deity or a dragon.

Of course, the Chinese happily accept the absence of a body on a *taotie*, and have a myth that explains this. It seems that the *taotie* was once wicked enough to eat human beings—its gluttony knew no bounds. As a punishment the gods decided to remove its body and leave it without any means of digesting food, and sentenced it to be displayed on food vessels as a warning to others not to overindulge.

Pulao

For many years it has been conventional to put dragons on tops of bells as a handle. It is not clear whether the *pulao* is a double beast rather like a pair of Siamese twins, or whether there are two *pulao* (Plate 20). A legend has grown up that these dragons have a roar that shakes the earth and the heavens, especially when attacked by their archenemy, the whale. According to Ban Gu (AD 32–92) in his *History of the Han* (*Han Shi*), 'There is the big fish in the sea called the whale, and the animal at the side of the sea is the *pulao*. It is afraid of the whale, and whenever the whale attacks the *pulao*, it roars. Whoever wishes to make a bell sonorous puts a *pulao* on it. The striker is the whale.' There are many examples of twin *pulao* handles to be seen on the magnificent bells on display at the Big Bell Temple in Beijing, the Dazhongsi (Plate 21).

Qiuniu

The head of a beast is sometimes carved on the top of two-stringed, moon-shaped fiddles. This is a *qiuniu*, and just as the *pulao* is associated with bells, the *qiuniu* is considered to be fond of music. It is another beast that has never had a body, and it can hardly be called a dragon unless one can accept that dragons can have only a head. Perhaps the *qiuniu* indulged in too much music and neglected its duties, and so, like the *taotie,* had its body removed?

Yazi

It is often claimed that a dragon's head with a wide-open jaw engulfing the blade was placed below the hilt of ancient Chinese swords and that this is a *yazi*. However, few, if any, swords with this attachment have been found. It is not uncommon, on the other hand, to find a dragon's head on the blades of ancient Japanese samurai swords. Some examples exist of decorative wooden halberds used at formal imperial Chinese ceremonies where a dragon's head has been carved as if holding the blade of the axe. This bodiless dragon is usually stated to be a *yazi* (sometimes written as *yazhai*) and is said to be a creature that loves to kill. If it is a son of the dragon, then it is yet another example of a dragon's head without a body (Plate 22).

Examples of dragons have been found on jade scabbards, but they are not typical *yazi*. The Art Gallery of the Chinese University of Hong Kong has some excellent examples in the Kwan Collection of jade scabbard chapes, scabbard slides, and sword guards. Most of these are dated to the Western Han dynasty (206 BC–AD 8). There are similar designs, also in jade, in the Dr Paul Singer Collection at the Arthur M. Sackler Gallery, Smithsonian Institution, Washington D.C., which are believed to be from the late Zhou dynasty and earlier. The dragons are carved in low relief with a lowered head, four legs, and a long curling tail. They have long horns which are elaborately voluted and hooked, probably to represent foliage, and are probably *guaizi* dragons.

Bian

Some lists of the sons of the dragon include a *bian*, and it is claimed that because of its ferocity it is placed on prison doors. However, as no ancient prisons have survived, with or without *bian* on the doors, this theory cannot be checked. It is also unlikely that any *bian* will be found on any contemporary prison door in China, and so we have another unsubstantiated claim. It is questionable that this son of the dragon, yet another with a head and no body, was ever used in prisons so the story will have to be taken at face value. It does not seem that the *bian* has ever appeared as an art motif.

There is also another body-less dragon, which is placed on the end of projecting beams under the eaves of palaces and temples in the Forbidden City. This is often stated to be a *bian*, but this particular dragon's head gets little publicity and is seldom discussed—often it is not even mentioned. It seems most unlikely that this *bian* has any connection with the fierce dragon's head that is alleged to be placed on prison doors. Again, the question of whether this is a son of the dragon is pure speculation.

Zhayu

As mentioned at the beginning of this Chapter, the *zhayu* is sometimes included in lists of the sons of the dragon. Visitors to the Forbidden City cannot fail to be impressed, perhaps even overawed, by the two huge gilded beasts guarding the southern entrance to the Imperial Garden, the Gate of Tranquil Longevity (Ningshoumen). They have awesome claws, an uplifted spiky mane, a fearsome dragon's head with flowing whiskers, an upright bushy tail, and a single short horn. These monsters are *zhayu* and they are intended to frighten the viewer: they certainly do that. Legend has it that *zhayu* resided in the yin world, the shades below the yang world of light, or in other words, in this world. It was believed that if the emperor had virtue—if he followed the Dao or Right Way—the *zhayu* would remain quiescent. If the emperor did not have virtue, it would appear and make protest. These statues were placed in the Forbidden City in late Qing times, whether as a hint to the emperor that he might perhaps be deficient in virtue is not known, but they were certainly put there as a reminder that a real *zhayu* might appear if he strayed too far from the straight and narrow. The emperor had to pass these fearful beasts every time he went to the garden, known in Ming times as the Palace Rear Garden, not that he spent much time in this hodgepodge of weird stone shapes and fossils. Perhaps he didn't like to be reminded of the potential dangers when he passed the *zhayu*? Incidentally, their favourite food is human beings, so when you get close to them, watch out!

Conclusion

So, what conclusion can be drawn about the nine sons of the dragon? Sadly one has to assume that these sons, whether nine or more, are only an idea or invention by self-styled 'authorities' with more imagination than knowledge. However, for many years the Chinese believed that the dragon had sons, and therefore sons there are, no matter how many.

6
Dragons on the Roof

A PROMINENT FEATURE of the buildings of the Forbidden City is the two open-mouthed, dragon-like finials on the ends of the roof ridge. Dominant finials had been used on Chinese buildings for many years: the very early ones were simply hook-shaped. These developed into a bird-headed shape, then into a fish, and finally the dragon was introduced. There were, of course, regional variations, and variations according to the date of erection, just as one might expect. However, refined, open-mouthed dragon designs have been found on surviving buildings of the Khitans (a Turko-Mongolian nomadic tribe originally from Manchuria, from which we get our word Cathay, for China) in the north-east erected during the Liao dynasty (907–1125), and on Song dynasty (960–1279) buildings.

The Office of Building of the Song Ministry of Public Works published a set of building standards for palace-style architecture, the *Yingzao fashi*, in the year 1103. The finials are referred to as *chiwei*, *chi* meaning owl-like and *wei* meaning tail. But these finials are certainly not owl-tailed, nor do they look remotely like owls, with or without an animal mouth. A better but still unsatisfactory name is found in several articles in the Palace Museum bulletins, where they are referred to as *da wen*, namely large (or great) animal-mouthed (things). However, this is merely a description, not a nomenclature. The precise name of the finial beasts, unfortunately, remains unknown.

Finials dated to the Jin (Jurchen) dynasty (1115–1234) show curious additions—the dragon is now provided with two stubby legs and has a sword handle projecting from its head.

Moreover, another dragon is carved on the side of the *da wen*'s head. In some cases a phoenix is carved on the other side, and a small dragon's head appears on the back of the finial, facing outwards.

An example of this last mentioned addendum can be seen on the Holy Mother (Shengmu) Hall at the Jin Ancestral Temple in Taiyuan, Shanxi province, said to have been built in the Northern Song dynasty, around 1025, and rebuilt in 1102. In Datong, also in Shanxi province, the library at the Huayan Monastery, built in 1038, the Main Hall of the Shanhua Monastery, built in 1060, and the Main Gate of this latter monastery all have these outward-gazing beasts. Another example can be found inside the hall of the Pure Land (Jingtu) Temple, in Yingxian, Shanxi province, built in 1124. This temple has a coffered ceiling on which beautifully carved celestial pavilions surround two imperial dragons. There are also dragon-fish facing inwards on the roof ridges, but there are small outwardly gazing beasts as well. This is most unusual, for the dragon-fish are almost invariably found without any outward-facing extras. The Manjusri Hall of the Foguang Temple, in Wutai, also in Shanxi, erected only a few years later, has no such beast. Similarly, there are no extra beasts on the side ridges of the Main Hall of the Shanhua Monastery in Datong, nor the Sanqing Hall, in Suzhou, Jiangsu province, both built in the twelfth century. However, the Yong Le Palace, which was built in the early thirteenth century (no connection with the Yong Le emperor), has dragon heads with distinct horns attached to the roof-ridge finials. Clearly, the practice of including a small dragon's head was not yet universal. However, from the mid-thirteenth century the outward-gazing dragon's head became standard and was always included (Plate 23). It has, however, attracted little attention and no explanation of precisely why it is there, or exactly what it represents, is available. The only indication of its name is that it is a *beishou*, literally 'the beast at the back'. Its inclusion obviously became traditional, yet its original purpose has been forgotten.

The triple-dragon design is carried to the ultimate on the Eastern Gate of the Great Wall at Shanhaiguan. The finial is made up of three beasts, all roughly the same size. One has a short scaly body with two crouching legs and a gaping mouth biting the ridge; the second is a writhing, serpentine dragon sitting near the top of the first beast's head; and the third, an upright beast, gazes outward, showing only the front part of its body and neck. This too has an open mouth. There is a sword clearly nailing the dragon to the beam. The construction date for the design at Shanhaiguan is not known.

It is interesting that it is rare to find four-legged traditional *long* dragons on roof ridges. However, examples can be seen on the Main Hall of the Kaiyuan Temple in Quanzhou, Fujian province. They are not biting the ridge, which continues beyond the dragons in a graceful upward curve. The temple was founded in the Tang dynasty (618–907) and was enlarged in the Song (960–1279), but it burned down during the Yuan dynasty (1279–1368) and was rebuilt during the reign of the Ming emperor, Yong Le (1403–1424). The restoration almost certainly followed the original design, however. Conventional dragons were used during the Qing dynasty (1644–1911), but only on temples under imperial patronage with Tibetan Lamaist overtones. An example of this can be found in the Forbidden City on the Pavilion of Rain Flowers, where four gilded bronze dragons face outward. This three-storied pavilion was built for the Qianlong emperor (1736–1795). There are similar *long* dragons to be found on the roof of the Xumifushou Tibetan Temple at the Summer Palace at Chengde, but they are in pairs, with the lower dragons looking outward and the upper dragons staring at the pinnacle.

The usual explanation for open-mouthed 'dragons' used as finials is that dragons were believed to be capable of gathering clouds and making rain, and they would guard the buildings against the deadliest enemy of wooden structures, fire. This is a somewhat simplistic explanation and ignores the sword handle. This, however, provides a significant clue as to the purpose of the *da wen*, as shown in a delightful Chinese myth that says that in ancient times the earth was beset with many demon dragons. Huangdi, the Yellow Emperor, decided that this had to end, so he sent Di Shi, who had magical powers, to dispose of these evil demons. This he successfully managed to do, killing all except those who were prepared to repent and do good deeds. Two of the worst demons, however, the Demon-Dragon of Concupiscence and Lust and the Demon-Dragon of Death, tried to avoid his attention and cleverly hid themselves. Di Shi, using his magical powers, realized they were still in existence and enticed them out by offering them sanctuary if they would perform deeds of usefulness. Enthusiastically they agreed, thinking they were being cunning. Di Shi then asked them to take the ridge beam of a temple in their mouths and fly with it to place it in position. They were happy to be given this task, knowing that it was important, for getting the ridge beam in place was one of the first requirements when constructing Chinese buildings. However, as soon as they had the beam in position, Di Shi took two magical swords and plunged them deeply into the two villainous beasts, leaving only the handle visible, and thus nailing them to the ridge beam. Di Shi, incidentally, is known as Indra to Buddhists.

There is an interesting parallel in a myth in esoteric Buddhism that says that Indra, the god of rain, was sent to conquer the non-Buddhist deities of Tibet. The essentials of this myth are identical with the story of Di Shi and swords were also plunged into the demons' bodies to nail them down.

The link between Daoism and Buddhism is intriguing, for the temples where the finial has a sword handle in the head of the open-mouthed *da wen* are invariably Buddhist. It is possible, therefore, that the dragon-like beasts on the roof ridges were considered to represent the triumph of Indra, the Buddhist god of rain, over evil dragons by means of the magical sword. The recognition of the achievement, and the sanctification of the victory, could be beneficial in emergencies caused by fire and might induce Indra to send down torrents of rain.

But what about the dragon displayed on the side of the evil *da wen*'s body? The temples were Buddhist, and Buddhists had plenty of reasons to be aware of the power of the emperor, for in the period 842 to 845 the Wuzong emperor instituted a brutal persecution of Buddhism. His antipathy stemmed from the refusal of the clergy to render homage to him as secular ruler. Under his orders more than 4,600 Buddhist temples and 40,000 shrines were destroyed, and 260,000 monks and nuns forced to return to lay life. This was a heavy blow to the religion, but Buddhism had permeated Chinese society so thoroughly that it could not be eliminated even by such vicious suppression. One hundred years later there was a considerable rise in the number of new temples being constructed. Simple discretion would dictate that at least some obeisance to the imperial dragon should be made, especially since his power was now omnipresent. Is it not possible that an imperial dragon carved on the bodies of the evil dragons could slyly suggest homage? The inscrutable monks could point out that the location of the imperial dragon on the head of the *da wen* clearly indicated its superiority. Furthermore, some ridge-beast finials even had a phoenix on the other side, for example at the Pool and Wild Mulberry (Tanzhe) Temple, just outside Beijing. Similar designs are to be found with both phoenix and dragon at Ordination Terrace (Jietai) Temple, near Beijing (Plate 24). These designs would tacitly reinforce the implication that imperial and secular power were not mutually exclusive. In some cases the imperial dragon is actually shown holding the evil dragon's horn in its claw. Did this not emphasize the point? And yet to those who wished to entertain the thought, it could imply that the imperial dragon was closely linked to the evil one. Incidentally, these finials are beautifully designed and executed, making the *da wen* on the buildings of the Forbidden City look like second-rate products.

The obeisance to the ruler is carried out with emphasis on temples at Suzhou, dating from the beginning of the second century, where an imperial dragon is often placed in the centre of the decorated south-facing roof-beam and a phoenix placed in a similar position on the north-facing side.

Regional variations in finial design occurred as one would expect, but around 1365 something astonishing occurred—all imperial roof furniture designs were suddenly frozen: right up to the present day, over 600 years later, the design of the *da wen* and other roof figures have not changed. It was for all the world as if there were a catalogue and the *da wen* and the other beasts, including the small roof figures, were ordered from that catalogue, and as if the catalogue was never once updated. Why did all the emperors keep to the same designs? I would venture an explanation.

It is known that it was necessary to create special tile works for the roof tiles of the Forbidden City, and most of these were set up in Beijing itself or in the nearby area, but probably the roof figures and beasts came from a specialist factory. Ceramic beasts, and ceramic tiles, were one of the few items that had to be purchased. Timber, and most other items, could be collected by State-paid soldiers and labourers, but ceramics had to be purchased in the completed form. The contracts must have been lucrative, to say the least, and the follow-up replacement business was equally so. Such contracts were issued continually from the mid-fourteenth century, not only until the end of the Qing dynasty, but even beyond that time. Is this not significant?

A set of regulations for building and furnishing Qing imperial palaces was issued between 1727 and 1750, more than 350 years after the palace was first built, and yet the design of the ceramic figures still remained unchanged. Curious. The regulations specified the prices to be paid for a wide range of items, including the roof ceramics, and their delivery charges. The price for a glazed *da wen* was more than ten times that of one in unglazed baked clay. Again curious, for one does not have to be an expert in ceramic figure production to conclude that the extra cost of glazing a baked clay moulding does not justify a tenfold increase in price.

Clearly, orders for *da wen* meant an attractive business for the factory owners. And when one considers the corruption in the Qianlong court, around the time the pricing regulations were issued it seems obvious that someone was authorizing the ceramic factory to make a nice profit from the supply and delivery of the ceramic figures. The Qianlong emperor approved the issue of the price list and so either he had the wool pulled over his eyes or he condoned the excessive payments. Back-handers to the Qianlong privy purse were not unknown, so he might not have been unhappy if excessive prices were being paid to the ceramic factory.

There was much importance attached to the *da wen* finials, particularly to the large ones. They were considered to be magical beasts, so an important official went to the factory to collect them. When they were mounted on the roof a special ceremony involving kowtowing and incense burning took place.

7
The Dragon and the Phoenix

No book on dragons would be complete without at least a brief mention of their relationship with the phoenix, for there is a widespread conviction that they were always linked, like the lion and the unicorn in English heraldry. This is not the case, however.

What exactly is a Chinese phoenix? By the end of the second millennium BC there was a mythical creature in the shape of a bird; the male was known as a *feng*, and the female was a *huang*. Later, these names were merged and *fenghuang* was taken as the generic word. In the absence of a meaningful translation of this name, Western writers fell back on the catch-all term phoenix.

In ancient times the *fenghuang* was considered as a symbol of fertility and was associated with the genitals. It gradually became beautified, idealized, and associated with the feminine gender, and developed into a symbol of beauty and a perfect being. Later still, it was elevated to the realm of love and into an emblem of light, luck, and happiness.

Various descriptions of the *fenghuang* arose. One authority stated that it had a rooster's head, a swallow's chin, a snake's neck, and a fish's tail, and that its feathers were very colourful, but of dark rich hues. Another authority relates a tale in which Tian Lao, a minister of the legendary Yellow Emperor, described the bird as having an upper body like a swan, a lower body like a *qilin* (the West usually calls this legendary beast a unicorn), and a turtle's back. He agreed, however, that it had a rooster's beak, a swallow's chin, a neck like a snake, and the tail of a fish. One self-styled authority and a court historian in the early Eastern Han dynasty by the name of Cai Heng stated, after a phoenix had apparently alighted at the home of the respected scholar Xin Shan, that there were five varieties: a blackish one called a *luan*, a whitish one called a swan, and three others that were either yellow, purple, or reddish.

The Chinese knew of many birds, but Western scholars seemed to be obsessed with phoenixes. Golden pheasants became 'red phoenixes', peacocks became 'green phoenixes', eagles became 'yellow phoenixes', swallows became 'white phoenixes', and magpies were styled as the 'black phoenix'.

In Chapter 2 of this book it is mentioned that the dragon was adopted by rulers as their personal symbol or emblem. However, the phoenix was not adopted by the empress as her emblem for many years. Like other women, she would use the phoenix as a decorative hair-embellishment and as a decorative emblem in her headdress. However, an empress wore dragon robes for formal occasions and not until the late Ming period (1368–1644) did the *fenghuang* occasionally appear on an empress's robes—always very discreetly of course, for it had to be subservient to the imperial dragon. Even then it was rarely used and it was only in Cixi's time in the late Qing dynasty (1644–1911) that the *fenghuang* appeared as part of the design on her empress-dowager robes.

A few ceramic plates and embroideries showing the dragon and phoenix together have been found, dated to the late Ming period, but it was not until the arrival of the Qing dynasty that dragon-phoenix designs became more commonplace (Fig. 7.1). Even then, the combination was rare.

The phoenix is found in many legends, one saying that a phoenix had scratched at the site of the first Ming emperor's father's grave. This auspicious act was taken to indicate approval of imperial power passing into his hands, a story perhaps circulated with his encouragement. There are several

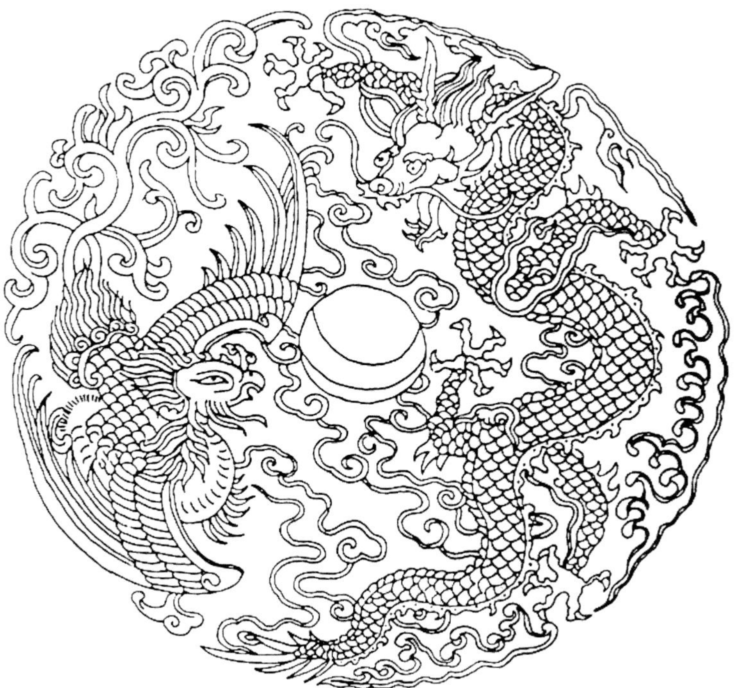

7.1 A Qing-dynasty roundel with the dragon and phoenix design, surrounding a central pearl.

legends where a phoenix opposes wicked dragons, but none with any connubial association with a dragon.

For many years, the *fenghuang* was used for decoration, often as a filler for corners of ceiling caissons. In the late Qing dynasty some beams in the Forbidden City were decorated with painted dragons facing these birds, but again always in low-key. It is unlikely that this was a deliberate attempt to link the emperor with his empress, for the symbol of marital bliss was two mandarin ducks. A dragon-phoenix design is almost unknown in imperial ceramic decorative panels and is seldom found on carved wooden or stone panels. The exception is that the 'skirt boards', or decorative panels, on the outer partition folding doors of the Hall of Vigorous Fertility (Jiaotaidian) in the Inner Court of the Forbidden City have dragons and phoenixes carved on them, but these represented beauty and were never intended to represent the empress. In Ming times this hall was used by emperors for bedding their females, and until Manchu (Qing) times, the empress's bed-space was in the larger hall to the north, in the Palace of Earthly Tranquillity (Kunninggong). There are also a few minor examples of dragons and phoenixes on beam paintings in the Forbidden City and on balustrade capitals alternating with carved dragon capitals, but never dragon and phoenix carvings as a pair.

The concept of a connubial association between the dragon and the phoenix is largely one developed by Western writers who have romantically and unrealistically assumed that there was affection and equality between a Chinese imperial husband and his wife.

Selected Chronology of Chinese History

Neolithic	*c*.7000–1600 BC
Hongshan culture	*c*.3500–2000 BC
Shang dynasty	*c*.1700–1027 BC
Zhou dynasty	*c*.1027–221 BC
Western Zhou	*c*.1027–771 BC
Eastern Zhou	770–221 BC
Spring and Autumn period	770–476 BC
Warring States period	475–221 BC
Han dynasty	206 BC–AD 220
Western Han	206 BC–AD 8
Eastern Han	25–220
Three Kingdoms period	220–280
Jin dynasty	265–420
Northern and Southern dynasties	386–589
Northern	386–588
Southern	420–589
Tang dynasty	618–907
Liao dynasty	907–1125
Song dynasty	960–1279
Northern Song	960–1127
Southern Song	1127–1279
Jin (Jurchen) dynasty	1115–1234
Yuan dynasty	1279–1368
Ming dynasty	1368–1644
Qing dynasty	1644–1911
Republic	1911–1949
People's Republic	1949–present day

Selected Bibliography

Chen Juan Juan (ed.), *Chinese Dragon Patterns*, text in Chinese, Hong Kong: Qing Gong Ye Publishing, 1994.

Chinese Academy of Architecture, *Ancient Chinese Architecture*, Beijing: China Building Industry Press, 1982.

Department of Architecture, *Historic Chinese Architecture*, Beijing: Qinghua University Press, 1985.

Destenay, Anne L. (tr.), *Nagel's Encyclopedia Guide: China*, Geneva: Nagel Publishers, 1978.

Doolittle, Revd Justus, *Social Life of the Chinese: A Daguerreotype of Daily Life in China*, London: Sampson Low, Son and Marston, 1868.

Eberhard, Wolfram, *A Dictionary of Chinese Symbols: Hidden Symbols in Chinese Life and Thought*, London: Routledge & Kegan Paul, 1986.

Garrett, Valery M., *Mandarin Squares*, Hong Kong: Oxford University Press, 1990.

———, *Chinese Clothing: An Illustrated Guide*, Hong Kong: Oxford University Press, 1994.

Goodridge, Carrington L. and Fang Chaoying (eds.), *Dictionary of Ming Biography*, two volumes, New York: Columbia University Press, 1976.

Hummel, Arthur W. (ed.), *Eminent Chinese of the Ch'ing Period*, Washington: United States Government Printing Office, 1943.

Jin Shoushen, *Beijing Legends*, Beijing: Chinese Literature, 1982.

Liang Ssu-ch'eng, *A Pictorial History of Chinese Architecture*, edited by Wilma Fairbank, Cambridge, Mass.: MIT Press, 1985.

Michaelson, Carol, *Gilded Dragons*, London: British Museum Press, 1999.

Rawson, Jessica, *Chinese Ornament: The Lotus and the Dragon*, London: British Museum Publications, 1984.

Ru Jingghua and Peng Hualiang, *Ancient Chinese Architecture*, Vienna: Springer-Verlag, 1998.

Schlegel, Gustaf, *Uranographie Chinoise*, La Haye-Leyden: Martinus Nijhoff, 1875.

Sirén O., *Chinese Painting*, Vol. II, New York: J. Cahill, 1958.

Wang Congren, *Dragon*, Hong Kong: Hai Feng Publishing Co. Ltd., 1996.

Weng, Wan-Go and Yang Boda, *The Palace Museum: Peking*, London: Orbis Publishing Ltd., 1982.

Williams, C. A. S., *Outlines of Chinese Symbolism & Art Motives*, New York: Dover Publications, 1976.

Yan Chongnian, *Beijing: The Treasures of an Ancient Capital*, Beijing: Morning Glory Press, 1987.

Yu Zhuoyun, *Palaces of the Forbidden City*, New York: Viking Press, 1984.

Zhang Dao Yi (ed.), *Chinese Dragons: Graphics and Rubbings*, text in Chinese, Beijing: Beijing Arts & Crafts Publishing House, 2000.

Index

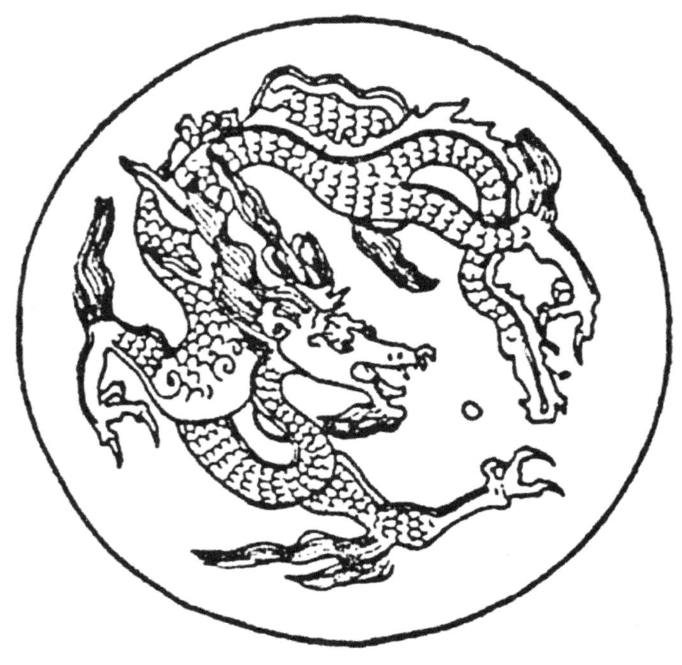

Song-dynasty three-clawed dragon on a tile end